STEWARDS OF THE MYSTERIES OF GOD

Stewards of the Mysteries of God

A Scriptural Study of Divine Stewardship

ERIC D. SMITH

Just1God
Publications

Stewards of the Mysteries of God

Published by Just1God Publications
Hilliard, Ohio 43026

Website: www.Just1God.org

Cover Design & Interior Layout by Lorie DeWorken
Edited by Courtney Campbell

All biblical quotes are from the King James Version unless otherwise noted.

ISBN 978-1-7359798-0-9 (print)

Italics, underlining, and bold in scripture quotations reflect the author's added emphasis.

ACKNOWLEDGEMENT

A special thanks to my wife, Bonnie, for encouraging me to write more than just sermons. She has not only allowed me the time to write, but also has helped me to create a sanctuary within our home for prayer and study. I also want to thank my Lord and my God, Jesus Christ, for loving me and calling me to be more than just an occupier of space on this planet. My love for Him and His Word propels me to go deeper in my walk with Him every day.

INTRODUCTION

There have been many books that I have purchased that, after reading the first couple of chapters, the writer seemed to have said everything of importance on his or her topic. After reading those first few chapters, there was so many "filler words and stories" that I had no interest to read any further. I do not want this book to be like one of those books. There is enough in the New Testament about the things of God that were "once hidden" and now revealed to the church that there is no need to use "filler words and stories".

I also have no intention of referring to some "mystery of God" from an ancient monk or unheard-of priest that would require extensive research for readers to verify. I am sure that there are already books on the market like that. I do not think God would hold us accountable as stewards for something that was never canonized (accepted as the written Word of God) or quoted within His Word. I will be keeping the "mysteries" discussed in this book to the revelations that the New Testament writers wrote about. Twenty-seven times the Greek word that is translated into the English word "mystery" or "mysteries" is used in the New Testament (KJV). If we are to be stewards and held accountable with these treasures that were once hidden, then we, as the body of Christ, need to learn, know, and share this knowledge. Ignoring the mysteries would be the same as the man who hid his talent in the earth until his master returned. No true believer would want to find themselves as the one being cast out into outer darkness for ignoring or hiding what has been given to us. So, join me now on this journey to safeguard our stewardship of the Mysteries of God.

TABLE OF CONTENTS

CHAPTER 1
Stewardship 1

CHAPTER 2
What is a Mystery? 9

CHAPTER 3
The Mystery of Christ in You 15

CHAPTER 4
The Mystery of God Manifested in the Flesh 25

CHAPTER 5
The Mystery of Gentiles Becoming Fellow-heirs 39

CHAPTER 6
The Mystery of the Resurrection 51

CHAPTER 7
The Mystery of Iniquity 61

CHAPTER 8
The Mystery of the Great Whore 73

CHAPTER 9
The Mystery of Christ and the Church 85

CHAPTER 10
Dear Pastor: If God Would Speak to You 95

CHAPTER 11
Conclusion – Building on a Solid Foundation 99

Afterword 107

Chapter 1
STEWARDSHIP

> "Let a man so account of us, as of the ministers of Christ,
> and stewards of the mysteries of God.
> Moreover it is required in stewards, that a man be found faithful."
> 1 CORINTHIANS 4:1-2

Many preachers throughout the centuries have taught on stewardship in reference to our money and our time, but few preachers, if any, have brought the teaching of the accountability required in stewardship into the realm of handling the mysteries that God has placed into the hands of the believers. Stewardship is often taught from two passages found in the New Testament Gospels of Matthew and Luke. In the Gospel of Matthew, Jesus tells of a man traveling into a far country and delivering unto his servants his goods while he is away. The word "goods" used here is referred to later as talents. The word "talent" comes from the Greek word *talanton,* which *Strong's Concordance* defines as "a balance", or "a certain weight, and thence a coin or rather, sum of money". *Strong's Concordance* continues its definition, saying, "A talent of silver in Israel weighed about 100 pounds (45 kg). A talent of gold in Israel weighed about 200 pounds (91 kg)." If the parable is referring to either silver or gold, then this was a very valuable treasure being left to the servants.

This parable begins with the phrase, *"For the kingdom of heaven is as a man travelling into a far country . . ."* (Matthew 25:14). Jesus, by referencing the Kingdom of Heaven, is giving us a direct allegory to Him handing us the incredibly valuable treasures of His Kingdom as He returns to Heaven. He is also telling us that when He returns for His Church, He is expecting His servants to have been faithful with the things that He has left to us. Inserted in this parable is found the often-quoted verse, *"His lord said unto him, Well done, thou good and faithful servant: thou hast been faithful over a few things, I will make thee ruler over many things: enter thou into the joy of thy lord"* (Matthew 25:21).

In the Gospel of Luke, the nineteenth chapter records the account of a certain nobleman leaving ten pounds to ten servants. Both words used in these parables, "talents" and "pounds", directly refer to money. The "pound" comes from the Greek word *mina. Strong's Concordance* gives us the meaning of "a certain weight". *Strong's Concordance* clarifies, "In the Old Testament, a weight of 300 shekels was one pound. In the New Testament, a weight and sum of money equal to 100 drachmae, one talent was 100 pounds." The amount given to the servants in Matthew's account was five talents, two talents and one talent. If it were silver, then it would be five hundred pounds, two hundred pounds and one hundred pounds, respectively. The amount, therefore, given to the servants in Luke's narrative (ten pounds to ten servants, or one pound each) was not as valuable as the amount given to the servants in Matthew's narrative. In other words, the amount given to the servants in Luke's narrative was approximately one percent of the value of that given in Matthew's account.

The lesson, though, in each of these parables is not focused on how much the servants valued the treasure, or on how much they received, but on the faithfulness of their stewardship. The master's reward to them upon his return was based on whether they used what the master gave them to benefit and build their master's kingdom. In Luke's account, although the value of the initial stewardship appeared smaller, it seemed that the entire accountability test was to prove how they would handle a much larger responsibility. Those that proved to be faithful servants in handling the pound were given whole cities corresponding to the increase of the pound. Those that were unfaithful in their stewardship of the pound were slain. In Matthew's account, the unfaithful servant was cast into outer darkness. In both accounts, we can see the significance and the consequence that Jesus places upon stewardship.

The lesson in each of these parables is not focused on how much the servants valued the treasure, or on how much they received, but on the faithfulness of their stewardship.

As mentioned at the beginning of this chapter, many preachers have taught on stewardship from these two accounts in reference to our money and our time, but both money and time are temporary commodities of this earthly life. Remember that Jesus said the Kingdom of Heaven is like these parables. Jesus taught in parables, or stories, to liken something people could understand to something that they may not have understood in any other form. Similarly, when Jesus taught about the sower and the seed, He did not intend for believers to become better farmers or gardeners. Since preachers do not use the parable of the sower and the seed to teach about gardening, why is it that they use the lessons of the talents and the pounds to teach that stewardship should be understood in direct reference to money or time? Even greater than the idea of money in these stories is the concept of what was done with that which was being entrusted into the care of the servants. There is something of much more value than both money and time that God has placed into the hands of the Church to take care of until He comes back! To teach the Church to be a better steward of our money from these passages would be as erroneous as teaching a believer to be a better gardener from the parable of the sower and the seed.

To teach the Church to be a better steward of our money from these passages would be as erroneous as teaching a believer to be a better gardener from the parable of the sower and the seed.

Paul mentions two responsibilities that we must give "account" of in this life. In the fourth chapter of 1 Corinthians, he writes that we are *"the ministers of Christ, and stewards of the mysteries of God"* (verse 1). The role of a minister that Paul is speaking of here is not referring to the position of a pastor or of a bishop (overseer) of a church. Instead, Paul uses a Greek word (*hypēretēs*) which means that of an "under-oarsman", or one that rows or toils. He is referring to someone who is rendering service to another, or anyone who aids another in any work. It is very important to understand that he is not referring to the role of a pastor or a bishop in this passage.

Only one time is the word "pastors" used in the King James Version of the Bible, and that occurrence is in Ephesians. Scripture states, *"And he gave some, apostles; and some, prophets; and some, evangelists; and some, pastors and teachers; For the perfecting of the saints, for the work of the ministry, for the edifying of the body of Christ:"* (Ephesians 4:11-12). Here, Paul is describing the fivefold ministry for the administration of the Church. The word translated here as "pastors" is from the Greek word *poimēn* and is translated as "shepherd" every other time it is used in the New Testament. *Strong's Concordance* defines this word as "he to whose care and control others have committed themselves, and whose precepts they follow". Then, in describing the function of each office in verse twelve, Paul mentions the purpose is *"for the work of the ministry"*. The word that Paul uses in verse twelve referring to ministry is from the Greek word *diakonia*, not the Greek word *hypēretēs*, as used in 1 Corinthians 4:1. *Diakonia* is where we get the English word deacon from. The word *diakonia* refers to a servant or worker within the administration or leadership of a church.

A common teaching in today's Church is that every believer is a minister. This is true; yet every believer is not a deacon, a pastor (shepherd), or a bishop. Every believer should be rendering service to our King and to His Kingdom. Every believer should understand that they are the under-oarsmen that are here to help the Church continue to move forward in the Great Commission. The shepherds (pastors) and bishops are here to give us protection and direction. The apostles and prophets are here to give us understanding and wisdom. The evangelists and teachers are here to herald the good news of salvation and dissect the deep things of God. If a believer has not stepped into one of these roles by a divine calling from God, then they need to be asking and seeking what they could do to be beneficial to the Kingdom as an under-oarsman. We all have a task to do in the Kingdom, whether we have been given a pound's worth of His treasure or a hundred pounds' worth of His treasure. When Jesus returns, our efforts to further His Kingdom and our faithfulness to our stewardship will be rewarded tremendously. The reward from our Master will be based on whether we use what the Master gave us to build His Kingdom. But if we do nothing with our lives and ministries after entering the Kingdom of God, it makes us unprofitable servants.

Every believer should understand that they are the under-oarsmen that are here to help the Church continue to move forward in the Great Commission.

When the master responded to the unprofitable servant in Matthew 25:27, he told him, *"Thou oughtest therefore to have put my money to the exchangers, and then at my coming I should have received mine own with usury."* The term "exchangers" is referring to the idea of a banker. Instead of burying a talent and never using it, if you do not know what to do with it, there will be someone that you can invest your talent with that can help you reap benefits. This concept that Jesus is giving us here is just like depositing your money in a bank and accruing interest. Jesus will not be pleased with believers who do nothing with what has been given to them. The ministry and stewardship that Jesus is really concerned with is much more than an offering or tithe that you give, or even the busy-ness of your day.

I still remember vividly the first few months after becoming a newborn "babe" in Christ. I was driving by our church and saw the pastor out mowing the grass. I could not at that time participate in spiritual leadership like him, but I could mow the grass. So, I became the church's grass mower. I was freeing up my pastor's time for the weightier matters he needed to attend to. We all need to learn to become ministers (under-oarsmen) in the Kingdom. We need to learn to serve others and learn to serve Christ.

If you are not sure about what to do in the Kingdom, then first answer the following questions. What do you do for a living? Do you repair computers? Maybe your talent could be used within the church with that. Can you cook, or can you pray? Maybe there is a need to help the sick or elderly in the church. If you are stumped on a talent within your life, ask your pastor if there is a need for just another hand at the oars. Although the parables of the talents and the pounds do not intend to really teach us about our stewardship of money and time, Paul is definitely writing that we will give an account as an "under-oarsman" (minister) within the Church. Not using our abilities for the Kingdom of God is just the same as burying our talent. Always strive for the "Well Done My Good and Faithful Servant" badge of honor!

Many preachers stop short, though, on the follow-through teaching of 1 Corinthians 4:1. We are to be ministers of Christ, but also, we are to be stewards of the mysteries of God! Although money and time are often the focus of stewardship teaching, there is no greater direct application of stewardship than when a command from the Word of God shows us of an eternal principle placed directly into our hands. When we become believers, we become stewards of the mysteries of God! The Apostle Paul states, *"Moreover it is required in stewards, that a man be found faithful"* (1 Corinthians 4:2). How much clearer could Paul be in this statement?

There is no greater direct application of stewardship than when a command from the Word of God shows us of an eternal principle placed directly into our hands.

We are stewards of the mysteries of God and the Master will someday ask how we did in this stewardship. But do most Christians even know what the "Mysteries of God" are that are being referred to here?

When a person comes into the understanding of salvation and makes that step of faith and commitment, the mysteries are often just as hidden to them at that moment of new birth as when it was hidden in ages past. If you have not understood the mysteries yet, then it is time to begin your diligent search, just as the woman searched her house for the lost coin (Luke 15:8), or the man finding the buried treasure in a field (Matthew 13:44) was willing to give his all to acquire it. It is time to explore what the Bible describes as a mystery and what has been placed into our hands to share with a lost and dying world. It is required by Jesus that we be found faithful in this matter.

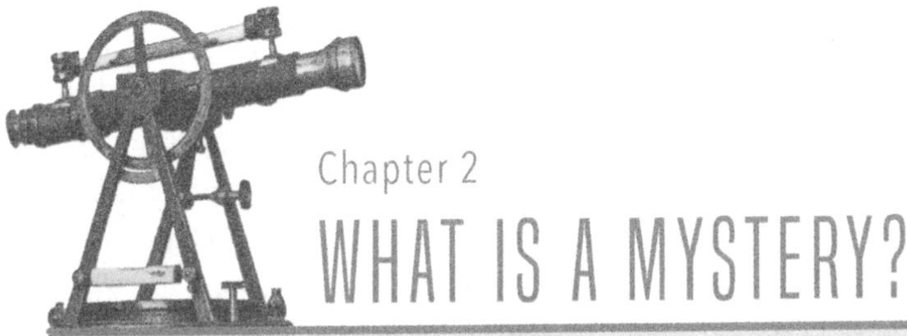

Chapter 2

WHAT IS A MYSTERY?

"Now to him that is of power to stablish you according to my gospel, and the preaching of Jesus Christ, according to the revelation of the mystery, which was kept secret since the world began,
But now is made manifest, and by the scriptures of the prophets, according to the commandment of the everlasting God, made known to all nations for the obedience of faith . . . ."
ROMANS 16:25-26

We are to be stewards of God's mysteries, and this necessitates our ability to understand the concept of what has been placed within our care. The word that is translated into the English word "mystery" or "mysteries" comes from the Greek word *mystērion.* An amazing twenty-seven times the writers of the New Testament use this Greek word. *Strong's Concordance* says the word is "from a derivative of *muo* meaning to shut the mouth." *Strong's Concordance* continues to say that it carries a connotation of "a secret or mystery . . . a hidden thing, something that is unknown or never spoken, uttered, or have been revealed". So, Paul is referring to believers as overseers of things that had been kept a secret, but now have been revealed; and, Paul tells us these mysteries have been *"made known to all nations for the obedience of faith"* (Romans 16:26).

This concept of mysteries that were once hidden since the world began and now being revealed to believers needs to be accepted as a biblical truth with consequences. The consequences I am referring to is what happens to unfaithful stewards . . . unfaithful stewards that have done nothing with the mysteries that have been given to the Church.

Transitioning from the Old Testament into the New Testament brought more than just grace. For example, the Old Testament prophet Isaiah revealed, *"For since the beginning of the world men have not heard, nor perceived by the ear, neither hath the eye seen, O God, beside thee, what he hath prepared for him that waiteth for him"* (Isaiah 64:4). But look closely at the following passage of scripture from the New Testament as Paul quotes this Old Testament passage from Isaiah:

> *But we speak the wisdom of God in a mystery, even the hidden wisdom, which God ordained before the world unto our glory: Which none of the princes of this world knew: for had they known it, they would not have crucified the Lord of glory. But as it is written, Eye hath not seen, nor ear heard, neither have entered into the heart of man, the things which God hath prepared for them that love him. But God hath revealed them unto us by his Spirit: for the Spirit searcheth all things, yea, the deep things of God. For what man knoweth the things of a man, save the spirit of man which is in him? even so the things of God knoweth no man, but the Spirit of God. Now we have received, not the spirit of the world, but the spirit which is of God; that we might know the things that are freely given to us of God.* (1 Corinthians 2:7-12)

Paul quotes the passage from Isaiah as he tells the believer that God is revealing to us the things that were hidden even to the Old

Testament writers like Isaiah. The Church is here upon this earth to do mighty works, and God is giving us mighty power, wisdom, and understanding through His Spirit in order to do these works. If the believer can understand what God is truly trying to do through the Church, we could then believe why Jesus declared the following statement in Matthew 11:11: *"Verily I say unto you, Among them that are born of women there hath not risen a greater than John the Baptist: notwithstanding he that is least in the kingdom of heaven is greater than he."* Through the Spirit of God, the Church has been given the revelation of mysteries that had been hidden from past generations, hidden even from the patriarchs and sometimes even the prophets of the Old Testament. Things that have been kept secret since the world began have been hand-delivered (or should I say Spirit-delivered) to the believer, being written down in the pages of the New Testament for us to know and become stewards of. We have been made stewards of revealed mysteries that even Isaiah did not know about. This is the stewardship of every believer, and we will be held accountable for what we do with this knowledge.

Things that have been kept secret since the world began have been hand-delivered to the believer, being written down in the pages of the New Testament for us to know and become stewards of.

Jesus also indicates to us in His parables that the mysteries of the Kingdom of Heaven are being revealed to us. For example, in reference to Jesus, the book of Mark comments on understanding mysteries:

And he said unto them, Unto you it is given to know the mystery of the kingdom of God: but unto them that are without, all these things are done in parables: That seeing they may see, and not perceive; and hearing they may hear, and not understand; lest at any time they should be converted, and their sins should be forgiven them. (Mark 4:11-12)

It would be hard to pinpoint exactly how many mysteries are being revealed to us through parables since many deal with things such as sowing and reaping, hidden treasures of the Kingdom, and so on. Every parable is supposed to reveal something about the Kingdom. The disciples were stumped by some of the parables that Jesus spoke to them, so they asked Him to explain them. My purpose in this book is to look at the things referred to as "mysteries" revealed by the New Testament writers and document them through scripture. The many parables that Jesus taught are covered by countless other authors which bring forth many valuable lessons.

Jesus indicates that every mystery that the Bible speaks of BELIEVERS should be able to understand. It is the non-believer that will not understand the mysteries of God. But God wants us, the believers, to not only know, but understand and apply His principles. So, that means we need to be studying, praying, and reading the Word. God does not want us to be ignorant of the knowledge that He puts forth for us to know.

Recognize that the root word of ignorant is the word *ignore.* People usually ignore something because something else takes precedence in their time or attention. The non-believer will not understand the mysteries of God; however, the "Distracted Believer" (if I can use my own coined phrase) will not either. If a believer is ignoring the Word of God because they are being distracted by entertainment, sports, sin, or even simply overwhelmed by the cares of this world, then ignorance of the Word and of the mysteries entrusted into their care will result. That type of believer has become a distracted believer. But God does not want us to be distracted, thereby becoming ignorant and allowing other things of this world to take precedence over the knowledge of His Word. Do not become distracted by the cares and the sins of this world, ignoring the vast riches and revelations held within the Word of God!

Paul, when writing about one of the mysteries, even pens these words, *"For I would not, brethren, that ye should be ignorant of this mystery . . ."* (Romans 11:25). God wants the mysteries which have been kept secret since the world began to be revealed to the believer. Those mysteries which have been kept secret have now been placed within our care. The revealed mysteries are the greatest treasures that the Church carries to reach a lost and dying world. This treasure of knowledge is what we will be held accountable for as stewards.

The following chapters discuss the mysteries of God. Some chapters will be longer than others. Some chapters will be more important for us to understand the mystery discussed. If you never understand Babylon the Great, it might not affect your salvation (unless you are being deceived by Babylon the Great). If you could never clearly explain the physics in the mystery of how in the twinkling of an eye our bodies will be changed, it probably, again, will not affect your salvation. But if you "ignore" the mystery that Paul speaks about in the first chapter of the letter to the Colossian Church (the next chapter of this book), then you will never be saved from eternal damnation. This is how important some of the mysteries are that have been entrusted to the Church that God wants us to share with the unsaved world.

Chapter 3

THE MYSTERY OF CHRIST IN YOU

"Whereof I am made a minister, according to the dispensation of God which is given to me for you, to fulfil the word of God;
Even the mystery which hath been hid from ages and from generations, but now is made manifest to his saints: to whom God would make known what is the riches of the glory of this mystery among the Gentiles; which is Christ in you, the hope of glory: whom we preach, warning every man, and teaching every man in all wisdom;
that we may present every man perfect in Christ Jesus."
COLOSSIANS 1:25-28

As Paul tells of one of the greatest mysteries revealed in the New Testament, he describes this mystery as one that *"hath been hid from ages and from generations, but now is made manifest to his saints"* (Colossians 1:26). As you will see through this study, when a writer such as Paul mentions something as a mystery, he is usually ready to explain the mystery. Here, Paul tells us that God wants to make known *"the riches of the glory of this mystery among the Gentiles"* (Colossians 1:27). When he uses the term "Gentiles", he is wanting us to understand that more than just the Church is to become aware of this mystery which was once hid, but he includes who the Church is to carry this knowledge to. The Church is to take the riches of the glory of this mystery unto the unchurched, even the non-Jew. The ultimate purpose of being a steward of this mystery is recorded in verse twenty-eight when it says, *"that we may present every man perfect in Christ Jesus."* Without the knowledge of this mystery, a man WILL NOT BE PERFECT in Christ Jesus.

***The ultimate purpose of being a steward of this mystery is recorded in verse twenty-eight when it says,* "that we may present every man perfect in Christ Jesus."**

Paul clearly reveals the mystery that had been hid from ages and from generations as he pens these words in the first chapter and twenty-seventh verse of Colossians, *"which is Christ in you, the hope of glory"*. Paul did NOT say that the mystery is Jesus Christ. He distinctly says the mystery is *"Christ in you"*. This is in direct reference to God filling a believer with His Spirit, which is often referred to in modern times as being "born again". The Old Testament writers had spoken about this promise that God had made to His people. One of the most obvious passages about God's promise is found in the book of Ezekiel:

> *A new heart also will I give you, and a new spirit will I put within you: and I will take away the stony heart out of your flesh, and I will give you an heart of flesh. And I will put my spirit within you, and cause you to walk in my statutes, and ye shall keep my judgments, and do them.* (Ezekiel 36:26-27)

Other passages of scripture referring to God putting His Spirit within man include Ezekiel 11:19-20 and Joel 2:28-29. It was from the book of Joel that Peter quotes on the Day of Pentecost in Acts chapter two when God pours His Spirit out upon the early church:

> *But this is that which was spoken by the prophet Joel; And it shall come to pass in the last days, saith God, I will pour out of my Spirit upon all flesh: and your sons and your daughters shall prophesy, and your young men shall see visions, and your old men shall dream dreams . . . .* (Acts 2:16-17)

Peter was referring to the spiritual experience that had just taken place in the second chapter of Acts, verses one through four. This spiritual experience is noted in great detail:

> *And when the day of Pentecost was fully come, they were all with one accord in one place. And suddenly there came a sound from heaven as of a rushing mighty wind, and it filled all the house where they were sitting. And there appeared unto them cloven tongues like as of fire, and it sat upon each of them. And they were all filled with the Holy Ghost, and began to speak with other tongues, as the Spirit gave them utterance.* (Acts 2:1-4)

Up until the time those believers who were gathered in the upper room *"were all filled with the Holy Ghost, and began to speak with other tongues, as the Spirit gave them utterance"*, the understanding of what God was promising (God putting His Spirit within them), and how God would bring it to pass, was still a mystery (Acts 2:1-4). Even the disciples had no idea how it was going to happen. They were just instructed by the resurrected Jesus that *"they should not depart from*

Jerusalem, but wait for the promise of the Father, which, saith he, ye have heard of me" (Acts 1:4). Only when it actually happened to them did they understand the dynamics of the promise and of the mystery. The reason Peter then quotes from the book of Joel is because the onlookers and the unbelievers were confused about what they were seeing and hearing. Some of the unbelievers even mocked the experience and accused them of being full of new wine (Acts 2:13). Unbelievers in the twenty-first century still mock this same Pentecostal experience; so, therefore, the believer, the steward of the mysteries of God, needs to stand up once again and proclaim the promise that God has made and is now fulfilling. It was important for Peter to wisely use his stewardship of the knowledge of God's mysteries in Acts chapter two, and, it is imperative for us to use this same knowledge *"that we may present every man perfect in Christ Jesus"* (Colossians 1:28).

***It was important for Peter to wisely use his stewardship of the knowledge of God's mysteries, and, it is imperative for us to use this same knowledge* "that we may present every man perfect in Christ Jesus".**

There is a passage of scripture in the Gospel of John that shows us even a learned Jewish ruler, trained in the scriptures of the Old Testament, did not understand how the promise was going to be fulfilled. The Gospel of John provides us with a vivid account of the story:

> *There was a man of the Pharisees, named Nicodemus, a ruler of the Jews: The same came to Jesus by night, and said unto him, Rabbi, we know that thou art a teacher come from God: for no*

> *man can do these miracles that thou doest, except God be with him. Jesus answered and said unto him, Verily, verily, I say unto thee, Except a man be born again, he cannot see the kingdom of God. Nicodemus saith unto him, How can a man be born when he is old? can he enter the second time into his mother's womb, and be born? Jesus answered, Verily, verily, I say unto thee, Except a man be born of water and of the Spirit, he cannot enter into the kingdom of God. That which is born of the flesh is flesh; and that which is born of the Spirit is spirit. Marvel not that I said unto thee, Ye must be born again. The wind bloweth where it listeth, and thou hearest the sound thereof, but canst not tell whence it cometh, and whither it goeth: so is every one that is born of the Spirit. Nicodemus answered and said unto him, How can these things be? Jesus answered and said unto him, Art thou a master of Israel, and knowest not these things?* (John 3:1-10)

Jesus is plainly teaching us that in order to see the Kingdom of God, a person must be born again. When it was evident that Nicodemus had no knowledge of this experience (it was a mystery to him), Jesus re-phrased His statement. He then said that in order to enter into the Kingdom of God, a person must be born of water and of the Spirit (John 3:5). Because of the Greek word that Jesus uses for water, He is not referring to the natural water surrounding the baby in the womb (*hydrōpikos* – the collection of fluids in different parts of the body). But Jesus uses a Greek word that refers to a body of water that has fallen as rain (*hydōr*) and now gathered as a river, fountain, pool, etc. Water baptism (which is complete immersion in water) in the name of Jesus Christ is necessary to enter into the Kingdom. (For further reading on water baptism, see Acts 2:38, Acts 8:12-16, Acts 10:44-48, Acts 19:1-6, and Romans 6:3-5.)

In this passage, Jesus is breaking down the born again experience by saying that a man must be born of water and of the Spirit in order to enter into the Kingdom of God. Repentance is paralleled with crucifying the flesh and dying to our carnal, sinful nature. Water baptism is paralleled as being buried with Christ (Colossians 2:12). Having the Spirit within us is paralleled to being resurrected or being given new life; like Christ was given:

> *Know ye not, that so many of us as were baptized into Jesus Christ were baptized into his death? Therefore we are buried with him by baptism into death: that like as Christ was raised up from the dead by the glory of the Father, even so we also should walk in newness of life. For if we have been planted together in the likeness of his death, we shall be also in the likeness of his resurrection . . . .* (Romans 6:3-5)

Understand also that the word "Spirit" that Jesus uses in John chapter three is translated from the Greek word *pneuma*. We get the English word pneumatic from this Greek word. A pneumatic tool is a tool that is operated by air. Jesus continues to use this word, *pneuma*, in verse eight and here it is translated into the English word "wind". Wind, like the Spirit, is something that is invisible (you can see particles picked up by the wind but not the wind itself) yet you can feel it and Jesus says you can hear the sound of it. He then tells us that *"so is every one that is born of the Spirit"* (John 3:8).

When God put His Spirit within the believers on the day of Pentecost, the thing that caught the crowd's attention was the sound that was coming from the upper room. The believers were all speaking in "other tongues". It was God that chose to use a sound when He poured out His Spirit. As mentioned previously, the disciples did not know what to expect as they were waiting for the promise of the Father, but it was this sound that caused the men gathered there in Jerusalem for the feast of Pentecost to be amazed and they marveled at what they heard. God was the one to choose again the sound of other tongues with this experience when the Gentiles received the infilling of the Spirit in Acts chapter ten. When Peter was questioned about preaching the message of salvation to the Gentiles in chapter eleven of Acts, it was the "speaking in other tongues" that Peter was able to use to confirm to the elders that it was the same experience that the Jews had from God. When the disciples of John the Baptist were met by Paul in Acts chapter nineteen, many years after the initial outpouring of the Holy Spirit, God was still using the sound of other tongues when the Spirit came to rest within the heart of the believer.

When God put His Spirit within the believers on the day of Pentecost, the thing that caught the crowd's attention was the sound that was coming from the upper room.

The mystery of Christ in you, which hath been hid from ages and from generations, was now being made manifest to his saints throughout every church. The early church accepted the occurrence of speaking in other tongues with the infilling of the Holy Spirit without question. It was the very thing that proved that the Gentiles had the same Holy Ghost experience as the Jews. And yet today, this mystery that had been hid from ages and from generations, revealed to the saints of the early church, is being hid once again by some within the modern church. When the contemporary pulpit preacher teaches that the *"Christ in you"* experience is received differently than what the Jews and the Gentiles of the book of Acts experienced, then the knowledge of the mystery once manifested to the early saints becomes buried and hidden once again.

If we are to be stewards of this mystery, then we should be preaching the same message of how God manifested this mystery in the early church. The uninformed masses of this world need to know the truth so they can be presented perfect in Christ Jesus. Without being born of the Spirit, they will never enter into the Kingdom of God. Many of the contemporary pulpits will even try to question whether the Pentecostal *"Christ in you"* experience is for us today. Paul lets us know that the same Spirit that raised up Christ from the dead will be raising us up from the dead. The Spirit residing within us is therefore a question of eternal death or eternal life. So, I will end this chapter by letting Paul answer the question of whether the *"Christ in you"* experience is for us today:

> *So then they that are in the flesh cannot please God. But ye are not in the flesh, but in the Spirit, if so be that the Spirit of God dwell in you. Now if any man have not the Spirit of Christ, he is none of his. And if Christ be in you, the body is dead because of sin; but the Spirit is life because of righteousness. But if the Spirit of him that raised up Jesus from the dead dwell in you, he that raised up Christ from the dead shall also quicken your mortal bodies by his Spirit that dwelleth in you.* (Romans 8:8-11)

The uninformed masses of this world need to know the truth so they can be presented perfect in Christ Jesus. Without being born of the Spirit, they will never enter into the Kingdom of God.

As stewards of the mysteries of God, we are not to hide this knowledge of *"Christ in you"* from a world that needs Jesus; and, we are not to change the message of how it was revealed and manifested in the saints of God. Being born again and entering into the Kingdom of God is not the act of coming forward at the end of a service and shaking a preacher's hand. In order to build the Master's Kingdom until He returns, faithful stewards of this mystery of *"Christ in you"* must preach the same born again experience of the infilling of the Spirit, evidenced by speaking in other tongues. Jesus said a person must be born of water and of the Spirit in order to enter into the Kingdom of God. Peter knew that the Gentiles had the same Holy Ghost infilling experience because *"they heard them speak with tongues, and magnify God"* (Acts 10:46). To reiterate, Paul described the mystery of *"Christ in you"* in Colossians 1:26-28:

> *Even the mystery which hath been hid from ages and from generations, but now is made manifest to his saints . . . which is Christ in you, the hope of glory: Whom we preach, warning every man, and teaching every man in all wisdom; that we may present every man perfect in Christ Jesus . . . .*

WE WILL BE UNPROFITABLE TO FALLEN HUMANITY, AND UNPROFITABLE TO OUR MASTER, IF WE REFUSE TO BE FAITHFUL STEWARDS OF THIS MYSTERY!

*If you have never experienced the powerful infilling of the Holy Ghost as mentioned in the book of Acts chapter two, evidenced by speaking in other tongues, please go to **www.Just1God.org** and click on the tab, "Church Search". There will be websites of organizations that can help you find churches in your specific area that are still being faithful in the stewardship of this powerful mystery revealed to the early church.

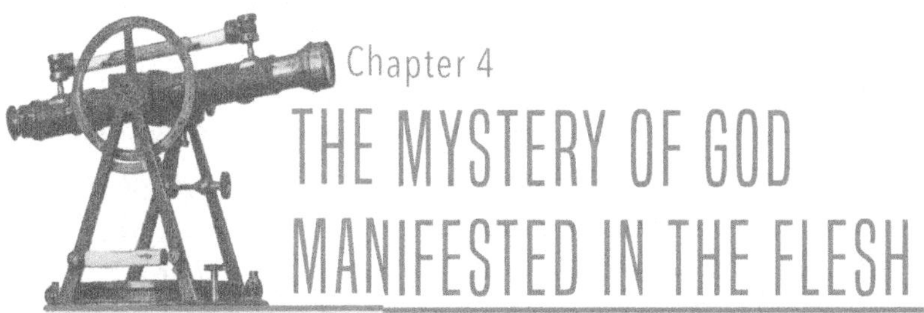

Chapter 4

THE MYSTERY OF GOD MANIFESTED IN THE FLESH

"And without controversy great is the mystery of godliness: God was manifest in the flesh, justified in the Spirit, seen of angels, preached unto the Gentiles, believed on in the world, received up into glory."

1 TIMOTHY 3:16

As God revealed to the Church the mysteries that had been hid from ages and from generations, the rulers of the darkness of this world and the spiritual wickedness in high places have continually worked to try to bury not just one, but every mystery once again. The Church's spiritual adversary (Satan) does not want us to comprehend and be faithful stewards of the mysteries . . . mysteries revealed to us in order to save a lost and dying world. The understanding of the mysteries can unlock the treasures of the Kingdom of God to help the lost of this world be transformed into the saints of the Living God. This is why the prince of this world wrestles so hard to keep the mysteries still a mystery to the Church. An ignorant Church becomes weak and harmless to the tricks of the deceiver. The wicked one does not even mind a person attending church if that church never preaches the true identity of Christ and the importance which that brings.

Paul charges Timothy in the second letter written to him to be prepared, no matter the circumstance. Paul advises him to be patient and bold:

> *Preach the word; be instant in season, out of season; reprove, rebuke, exhort with all longsuffering and doctrine. For the time will come when they will not endure sound doctrine; but after their own lusts shall they heap to themselves teachers, having itching ears; And they shall turn away their ears from the truth, and shall be turned unto fables.* (2 Timothy 4:2-4)

We live in a day when pulpiteers are applauded for giving cute stories of faith and of increased blessings while overlooking matters of sound doctrines that bring true salvation.

Not understanding the true identity of Jesus has proven throughout the centuries to keep new believers from following through with one of the simple steps involved in salvation – taking on the name of Jesus in water baptism. Without understanding this mystery that Paul is communicating to Timothy, some believers have only titles called over them in water baptism and not the NAME of Jesus Christ.

Not understanding the true identity of Jesus has proven throughout the centuries to keep new believers from following through with one of the simple steps involved in salvation – taking on the name of Jesus in water baptism.

Again, some contemporary pulpits may want to argue that this is of no significance, but Acts 4:12 declares, *"Neither is there salvation in any other: for there is none other name under heaven given among men, whereby we must be saved."* Peter commands the people in Acts 2:38 to *"be baptized every one of you in the name of Jesus Christ for the remission of sins . . . ."* Paul actually re-baptizes the followers of John the Baptist (Acts 19:1-6), this time using the name of Jesus since the name was not used in water baptism before the crucifixion of Jesus.

The remission (removal) of our sins is of utmost importance to our salvation; so, therefore, the name of Jesus in water baptism is doctrinally indispensable since there is salvation in no other name. Because the disciples knew the mystery of His identity, they understood the "name" (note it is singular) of Matthew 28:19 and baptized everyone in the name of Jesus Christ. They understood that "Father", "Son," and "Holy Ghost" were just titles and not a name. The true identity of Christ is where Paul is going with his declaration in 1 Timothy 3:16. After Paul instructs Timothy at the beginning of this chapter about the importance of purity and integrity in the leadership of the Church, he then makes the statement, *". . . and without controversy great is the mystery of godliness."* By saying "without controversy", he is telling us that no one of integrity in leadership authority would argue against the fact that this mystery is of mega-importance. (The word "great" comes from the Greek word *megas.*)

Paul describes this mystery as *"the mystery of godliness"* (1 Timothy 3:16). The word which is translated into the English word "godliness" is from the Greek word *eusebeia. Strong's Concordance* defines this word as piety towards God. *Merriam-Webster Dictionary* defines piety as "showing reverence for deity and devotion to divine worship". Paul, therefore, is declaring that a mystery exists in the Christian's worship of their God. Like in the last chapter, let me again state what Paul is NOT saying. He is not saying, "Great is the mystery of God." Are you catching that? The mystery is in the FOCUS of our worship. Stay with me in that thought and I will return to it again. But as I stated earlier, when a writer mentions something as a mystery, he is usually ready to explain the mystery. Paul is ready to explain this Christ that the Christians worship. Paul declares six truths unto Timothy about our God that is now forever documented for ages to come. He tells us that *"God was manifest in the flesh, justified in the Spirit, seen of angels, preached unto the Gentiles, believed on in the world, received up into glory"* (1 Timothy 3:16).

Paul declares six truths unto Timothy about our God that is now forever documented for ages to come.

The only Deity that these six truths can all be said of is Jesus Christ Himself. But before claiming the identity of the subject of Paul's declaration as Jesus, it would be helpful to understand the true grammatical subject from the Greek text. A few of the modern translations of the Bible have tried to make a change in the "who" these truths are referring to. The New Living Translation (NLT) and The Living Bible (TLB) use the word "Christ" as the subject of the six truths. Several other modern translations, including the New International Version (NIV), uses an ambiguous "He" to denote the focus of these truths. For the steward of the mysteries of God to truly understand this mystery, you must look at the original Greek word that was used as the grammatical subject. The grammatical subject was not the Greek word *Christos*, in which we get the English word Christ. Nor was it *ekeinos*, in which we get the English word He, like in John 1:8 describing John the Baptist, *"He was not that Light, but was sent to bear witness of that Light."* Sometimes the "He" is an implied subject that was already referred to, like two verses later in John 1:10, now referring to Jesus, *"He was in the world, and the world was made by him, and the world knew him not."* The word that Paul uses in 1 Timothy 3:16 as the subject of the six truths is *theos*. This is the Greek word that translates into the English word for *God!*

If Paul had said that *Christos* was manifested in the flesh, it would be easy for some believers to think of the second person of a trinity coming down in flesh form. Even with the ambiguous "He" manifesting himself in the flesh, it would be easy for a reader to assume whatever he thought of the Godhead. But Paul specifically uses the Greek word *theos* here. It was God that was manifested in the flesh. Unfortunately, this is still a mystery that eludes many Christians today. Great amounts of time and effort have gone into the construction of an idea of a trinitarian God. A three "person" Being, no matter how it is taught, still comes out to being three deities or Gods. Neither the Old Testament writers, nor the New Testament writers, ever wrote about or sanctioned the theory of three Gods (or "three Gods" in one).

But Paul specifically uses the Greek word* theos *here. It was God that was manifested in the flesh.

The very foundation of the Jewish belief is that there is only ONE GOD. This was firmly established in the Jewish faith because of the commandment that God gave to them in Deuteronomy 6:4-9:

> *Hear, O Israel: The LORD our God is one Lord: And thou shalt love the LORD thy God with all thine heart, and with all thy soul, and with all thy might. And these words, which I command thee this day, shall be in thine heart: And thou shalt teach them*

diligently unto thy children, and shalt talk of them when thou sittest in thine house, and when thou walkest by the way, and when thou liest down, and when thou risest up. And thou shalt bind them for a sign upon thine hand, and they shall be as frontlets between thine eyes. And thou shalt write them upon the posts of thy house, and on thy gates.

It was the declaration that there is only one Lord, and the commandment to talk, walk, and live this concept every day, that implanted this belief of one God into their hearts and minds.

Both the Old Testament and New Testament writers reinforce the fact that there is just one God and it was this only God of Heaven that came down in flesh form to become our Savior. This is the truth about God that Paul spoke about in 1 Timothy 3:16 when he said that God was manifest in the flesh. *Strong's Concordance* defines the word *manifest* as "to make visible or known what has been hidden or unknown, to manifest, whether by words, or deeds, or in any other way." This action of "manifestation" was able to make visible (in the form of a human) something that had been invisible (the Spirit). God is a spirit (John 4:24). A spirit is invisible (like the *pneuma* Jesus referred to). However, when Paul speaks of the invisible God in another passage to the Colossians, it is very interesting that he speaks of Jesus as being the image of the invisible God, and speaks of Jesus as being the creator of all things and that in Jesus should ALL fullness (not one third) dwell.

Both the Old Testament and New Testament writers reinforce the fact that there is just one God and it was this only God of Heaven that came down in flesh form to become our Savior.

Look closely at these passages in the book of Colossians. For example, Colossians 1:14-19 exemplifies the nature of Jesus Christ as the Living God:

> *In whom we have redemption through his blood, even the forgiveness of sins: Who is the image of the invisible God, the firstborn of every creature: For by him were all things created, that are in heaven, and that are in earth, visible and invisible, whether they be thrones, or dominions, or principalities, or powers: all things were created by him, and for him: And he is before all things, and by him all things consist. And he is the head of the body, the church: who is the beginning, the firstborn from the dead; that in all things he might have the preeminence. For it pleased the Father that in him should all fulness dwell.*

Jesus is the image or icon (*eikon* – the Greek word used here) of the invisible, by him were all things created (Jesus is the Creator of ALL things including thrones, dominions, principalities and powers in Heaven and in earth), and in Him ALL FULLNESS dwells.

The believer needs to understand that when the Bible mentions the Father (as in verse nineteen), the Spirit or the Holy Spirit (or Holy Ghost), it is always referring to the invisible deity of the Almighty. When the Holy Ghost overshadowed Mary for her to conceive, it was still the Father (the Almighty) that the Bible is referring to. When the Bible mentions Jesus, the Christ, or the Son, the writer is referring to the flesh that was born in Bethlehem. Understanding this will help you comprehend the mystery of our worship of the fleshly form of Jesus.

Now, let me return to the statement that Paul made to Timothy. Paul describes this mystery as *"the mystery of godliness"*. The word which is translated into the English word "godliness" is from the Greek word *eusebeia. Strong's Concordance* defines this word as piety towards God. *Merriam-Webster Dictionary* defines piety as "showing reverence for deity and devotion to divine worship". Paul, therefore, is declaring that a mystery exists in the object of the Christian's worship. The mystery is in the focus of our worship – a man, Jesus. Since we are commanded to not worship other gods or man (Exodus 20:3, Exodus 34:14, Revelation 19:10, Revelation 22:8-9), there is a great mystery of why believers would worship this human called Jesus. The mystery is contained in the fact that our Creator robed Himself in human form and the invisible God became manifested to the human eye.

When we worship Jesus, we are worshipping the Almighty God who came to earth as a man and AS OUR SAVIOR. That is why *"great is the mystery"* of the Christian's devotion to, and worship of, Jesus. He was not just mere flesh. What was kept secret from generations and ages past revealing how the Almighty was going to become our Savior is now plainly revealed in the New Testament. Paul was not telling Timothy anything new about Jesus, but he does forever document for the ages to come why we worship Jesus. Jesus was *THEOS "manifest in the flesh, justified in the Spirit, seen of angels, preached unto the Gentiles, believed on in the world, received up into glory"* (1 Timothy 3:16). Understanding the true identity of Jesus Christ will help us worship Him more genuinely and help us to obey the commandment to be baptized in His name, becoming passionate about the importance of the name of Jesus.

Paul was not telling Timothy anything new about Jesus, but he does forever document for the ages to come why we worship Jesus.

The Old Testament is full of references to the One Almighty God of Heaven becoming our Savior, and persistently tells us that He will not give His Glory unto another. In other words, God Almighty will not give His Glory to anyone or anything else. Isaiah speaks extensively of this. The following verses are passages that allow us to see into the prophecies of the coming Savior, the Almighty robing Himself in flesh. The word "Lord", which is used in these passages, is from the Hebrew word *YHWH.* The Hebrew writers would not fully write out the name of God in reverence to His holy name, so they always left the vowels out of His name, leaving us to speculate the name if spelled out. But as we translate today, it is translated as LORD, and the name is usually referred to as Yahweh or Jehovah. The word "God" that we see in these passages is from the Hebrew word "*El*", or "*Elohim*". Listen to what Isaiah says about the coming Redeemer and Savior:

> *For I am the LORD thy God, the Holy One of Israel, thy Saviour: I gave Egypt for thy ransom, Ethiopia and Seba for thee.* " (Isaiah 43:3)

> *Ye are my witnesses, saith the LORD, and my servant whom I have chosen: that ye may know and believe me, and understand that I am he: before me there was no God formed, neither shall there be after me. I, even I, am the LORD; and beside me there is no saviour. I have declared, and have saved, and I have shewed, when there was no strange god among you: therefore ye are my witnesses, saith the LORD, that I am God. Yea, before the day was I am he; and there is none that can deliver out of my hand: I will work, and who shall let it? Thus saith the LORD, your redeemer, the Holy One of Israel; For your sake I have sent to Babylon, and have brought down all their nobles, and the*

Chaldeans, whose cry is in the ships. I am the LORD, your Holy One, the creator of Israel, your King. (Isaiah 43:10-15)

I, even I, am he that blotteth out thy transgressions for mine own sake, and will not remember thy sins. (Isaiah 43:25)

Fear ye not, neither be afraid: have not I told thee from that time, and have declared it? ye are even my witnesses. Is there a God beside me? yea, there is no God; I know not any. (Isaiah 44:8)

Thus saith the LORD, thy redeemer, and he that formed thee from the womb, I am the LORD that maketh all things; that stretcheth forth the heavens alone; that spreadeth abroad the earth by myself. (Isaiah 44:24)

I am the LORD, and there is none else, there is no God beside me: I girded thee, though thou hast not known me: That they may know from the rising of the sun, and from the west, that there is none beside me. I am the LORD, and there is none else. (Isaiah 45:5-6)

For thus saith the LORD that created the heavens; God himself that formed the earth and made it; he hath established it, he created it not in vain, he formed it to be inhabited: I am the LORD; and there is none else. (Isaiah 45:18)

Tell ye, and bring them near; yea, let them take counsel together: who hath declared this from ancient time? who hath told it from that time? have not I the LORD? and there is no God else beside me; a just God and a Saviour; there is none beside me. Look unto me, and be ye saved, all the ends of the earth: for I am God, and there is none else. I have sworn by myself, the word is gone out of my mouth in righteousness, and shall not return, That unto me

> *every knee shall bow, every tongue shall swear. Surely, shall one say, in the LORD have I righteousness and strength: even to him shall men come; and all that are incensed against him shall be ashamed.* (Isaiah 45:21-24)

> *For mine own sake, even for mine own sake, will I do it: for how should my name be polluted? and I will not give my glory unto another. Hearken unto me, O Jacob and Israel, my called; I am he; I am the first, I also am the last.* (Isaiah 48:11-12)

Look again at Isaiah 45:23. God says that *"unto me every knee shall bow, every tongue shall swear."* This is what Paul quotes in Philippians 2:9-11 as he gives honor to Jesus:

> *Wherefore God also hath highly exalted him, and given him a name which is above every name: That at the name of Jesus every knee should bow, of things in heaven, and things in earth, and things under the earth; And that every tongue should confess that Jesus Christ is Lord, to the glory of God the Father.*

Since God will not give His glory unto another, the passage in Philippians can only be true if Jesus is the One True God of the Old Testament. The fleshly manifestation, life, and sacrifice of Jesus bring glory back to the Spirit, which is the Father. The name of Jesus was actually commanded by the angel to be given to the child born to Mary (Matthew 1:21, Luke 1:31).

Since God will not give His glory unto another, the passage in Philippians can only be true if Jesus is the One True God of the Old Testament.

Matthew also brings forth a quote from Isaiah 7:14 when he says, *"Behold, a virgin shall be with child, and shall bring forth a son, and they shall call his name Emmanuel, which being interpreted is, God with us"* (Matthew 1:23). Furthermore, the name Jesus literally means "Jehovah, Our Salvation". The name "Jesus" is actually the Greek translation of the Hebrew name "Yeshua". From the Hebrew language, *Yeshua* means "*YHWH* saves us". *Yeshua* is mentioned twice in Isaiah 12:2: *"Behold, God is my salvation; I will trust, and not be afraid: for the LORD Jehovah is my strength and my song; he also is become my salvation."* It is the word "salvation" that comes from the Hebrew word *Yeshua.* If these passages that mention *Yeshua* were to be translated into the Greek and then English, it would be easy to see that it could read, "Behold, God is my Jesus; I will trust, and not be afraid: for the LORD Jehovah is my strength and my song; he also is become my Jesus."

This is also why Isaiah can prophesy in Isaiah 9:6 about the coming birth of Jesus in Bethlehem. This powerful scripture records the prophecy of Isaiah:

> *For unto us a child is born, unto us a son is given: and the government shall be upon his shoulder: and his name shall be called Wonderful, Counsellor, The mighty God, The everlasting Father, The Prince of Peace.* (Isaiah 9:6)

He can be called *"the mighty God"* and *"the everlasting Father"* because the child being born was the mighty God and the everlasting Father being manifested in the flesh. Paul additionally tells us, *"To wit, that God was in Christ, reconciling the world unto himself, not imputing their trespasses unto them; and hath committed unto us the word of reconciliation"* (2 Corinthians 5:19).

Whether you refer to the God of the Old Testament as Jehovah or YAHWEH, there is still but One God, not a triune God. And to this One God will every knee bow and every tongue confess that He is Lord. Jesus Himself declares that He is the Almighty, stating, *"I am Alpha and Omega, the beginning and the ending, saith the Lord, which is, and which was, and which is to come, the Almighty"* (Revelation 1:8).

This chapter (in this book) began with Paul telling Timothy how great (mega) this mystery is. As Paul writes to the Colossian Church, he again mentions a mystery, but this time he describes a *"mystery of God, and of the Father, and of Christ"* (Colossians 2:2). He then tells them that in this mystery are hid all the treasures of wisdom and knowledge (Colossians 2:3). He proceeds to instruct them to stay stablished in the faith and not to be beguiled. This is followed up by a warning not to be "spoiled" (Colossians 2:7-8). The word that Paul uses that is translated as "spoil" is a Greek word that means "to lead away from". It is interesting that Paul warns against philosophy, vain deceit, tradition of men, and rudiments of the world, and then links this warning to a declaration of truth that in Jesus dwells ALL THE FULNESS OF THE GODHEAD bodily (Colossians 2:8-10). Paul is telling us that the philosophies, the deceit, and the traditions of men are trying to lead us away from the truth that in Jesus dwells all the fullness of the Godhead. He then adds that we are COMPLETE in Him (Jesus). Jesus is ALL that we need. Jesus is EVERYTHING that we need. Continually in the Old Testament, the basic foundation is laid down for us that there is only one God. It is the traditions of men that are trying to teach us something different. To end this chapter, I will let Paul tell you what he told the believers of Colossi almost two thousand years ago:

> *For I would that ye knew what great conflict I have for you, and for them at Laodicea, and for as many as have not seen my face in the flesh; That their hearts might be comforted, being knit together in*

love, and unto all riches of the full assurance of understanding, to the acknowledgement of the mystery of God, and of the Father, and of Christ; In whom are hid all the treasures of wisdom and knowledge. And this I say, lest any man should beguile you with enticing words. For though I be absent in the flesh, yet am I with you in the spirit, joying and beholding your order, and the stedfastness of your faith in Christ. As ye have therefore received Christ Jesus the Lord, so walk ye in him: Rooted and built up in him, and stablished in the faith, as ye have been taught, abounding therein with thanksgiving. Beware lest any man spoil you through philosophy and vain deceit, after the tradition of men, after the rudiments of the world, and not after Christ. For in him dwelleth all the fulness of the Godhead bodily. And ye are complete in him, which is the head of all principality and power . . . . (Colossians 2:1-10)

Paul is telling us that the philosophies, the deceit, and the traditions of men are trying to lead us away from the truth that in Jesus dwells all the fullness of the Godhead.

*Acts 4:12 declares unto us that *"Neither is there salvation in any other: for there is none other name under heaven given among men, whereby we must be saved."* If you have never been baptized in the name of Jesus Christ for the remission of your sins, or have only been baptized with the titles of Father, Son, and Holy Ghost, or, even unsure of your water baptism, please go to **www.Just1God.org** and click on the tab, "Church Search". There will be websites of organizations that can help you find churches in your specific area that are still being faithful in the stewardship of this powerful mystery revealed to the early church.

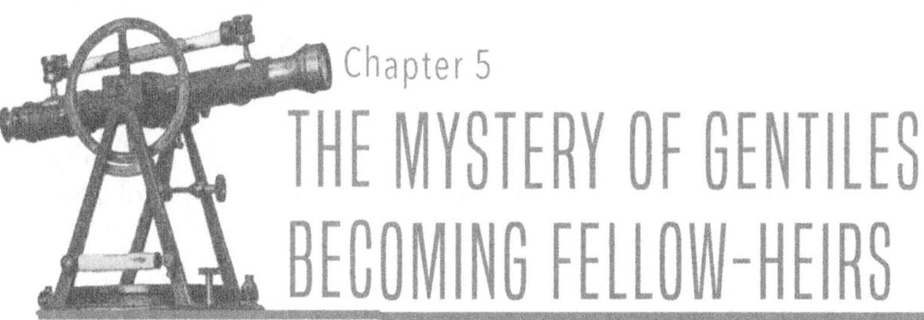

Chapter 5
THE MYSTERY OF GENTILES BECOMING FELLOW-HEIRS

"For this cause I Paul, the prisoner of Jesus Christ for you Gentiles, If ye have heard of the dispensation of the grace of God which is given me to you-ward: How that by revelation he made known unto me the mystery; (as I wrote afore in few words, Whereby, when ye read, ye may understand my knowledge in the mystery of Christ) Which in other ages was not made known unto the sons of men, as it is now revealed unto his holy apostles and prophets by the Spirit; That the Gentiles should be fellowheirs, and of the same body, and partakers of his promise in Christ by the gospel: Whereof I was made a minister, according to the gift of the grace of God given unto me by the effectual working of his power. Unto me, who am less than the least of all saints, is this grace given, that I should preach among the Gentiles the unsearchable riches of Christ; And to make all men see what is the fellowship of the mystery, which from the beginning of the world hath been hid in God, who created all things by Jesus Christ. . . ."

EPHESIANS 3:1-9

With this chapter, several of the "mysteries" mentioned in the New Testament come together to show that God had originally worked through the Jewish people, but His intent was always to bring the Gentile (a term referring to the non-Jew) people into the promise of salvation. As we live in the twenty-first century, it might be hard for us to comprehend that the very first Christians never thought of the Gentiles as being capable of God's promise of salvation. Today, the Christian Church is predominantly made up of Gentile believers. However, in the tenth chapter of the book of Acts, God had to do some strong persuading in order to get Peter (a Jew) to go to Cornelius (a Gentile) and preach to him and his household about Jesus Christ.

In verses one through eight of Acts chapter ten, God had heard the prayers of this Gentile named Cornelius. Cornelius was instructed by an angel to send men to Joppa to a specific house by the seaside to call for Peter so Peter could preach to him and his household the gospel. Cornelius listening to the angel and sending the men to fetch Peter actually seems to be the easy part of this story of Cornelius' salvation journey. The hard part was going to get a preacher, who was Jewish, to enter into a Gentile's home and preach to him. When Peter was persuaded by the Spirit to go with the men sent to Joppa for him, Peter stated the following comment while inside Cornelius' home, *"Ye know how that it is an unlawful thing for a man that is a Jew to keep company, or come unto one of another nation; but God hath shewed me that I should not call any man common or unclean"* (Acts 10:28).

If we could only accept and publicize ALL OF THE MYSTERIES that have been placed into the hands of the Church as easily as we do this one revelation, it would be so easy to achieve the **"Well done, thou good and faithful servant".**

Though we accept the Gentile converts without a thought today, it would not have been an acceptable concept during the first few years of Christianity. If we could only accept and publicize ALL OF THE MYSTERIES that have been placed into the hands of the Church as easily as we do this one revelation, it would be so easy to achieve the *"Well done, thou good and faithful servant"* (Matthew 25:21-23).

Look again at Ephesians chapter three and see how easily Paul is ready to disclose the mystery that was once hidden from generations past but now is revealed to him and to the Church:

> *How that by revelation he made known unto me the mystery . . . Which in other ages was not made known unto the sons of men, as it is now revealed unto his holy apostles and prophets by the Spirit; That the Gentiles should be fellowheirs, and of the same body, and partakers of his promise in Christ by the gospel* . . . . (Ephesians 3:3-6)

Several other places in the New Testament it mentions a mystery that points right back to the inclusion not only of the Gentiles, but of all of mankind. In a few of these scriptures, it refers to the *"mystery of His Will"*. We need to realize that it is God's Will that all of mankind be saved and come to the understanding of the grace and mercy that is being offered to all that have come short of the glory of God. This chapter started with Ephesians chapter three, but Paul had already expressed the revelation of this *"mystery of His Will"* earlier in his writing to the people at Ephesus. The first chapter of Ephesians expounds on this:

> *In whom we have redemption through his blood, the forgiveness of sins, according to the riches of his grace; Wherein he hath abounded toward us in all wisdom and prudence; Having made known unto us the mystery of his will, according to his good pleasure which he hath purposed in himself: That in the dispensation of the fulness*

of times he might gather together in one all things in Christ, both which are in heaven, and which are on earth; even in him: In whom also we have obtained an inheritance, being predestinated according to the purpose of him who worketh all things after the counsel of his own will: That we should be to the praise of his glory, who first trusted in Christ. (Ephesians 1:7-12)

We need to realize that it is God's Will that all of mankind be saved and come to the understanding of the grace and mercy that is being offered to all that have come short of the glory of God.

According to the scriptures stated above, this *"mystery of His Will"* is to be accomplished in *"the dispensation of the fullness of times"* (Ephesians 1:10). Galatians 4:4-5 speaks of God manifest in flesh: *"But when the fulness of the time was come, God sent forth his Son, made of a woman, made under the law, To redeem them that were under the law, that we might receive the adoption of sons."* In the Old Testament, God promised that all the families of the earth would be blessed through Abraham (Genesis 12:3). Abraham's lineage eventually became known as Hebrews but was also called Jews in certain places of the Bible. It was through Abraham's faith and belief in God that it was accounted to him for righteousness (Galatians 3:6, Romans 4:3). So, although the law came through the Jewish nation, the law was only to be a schoolmaster to show us that we are sinners in need of a Savior. For example, Galatians chapter three, verses twenty-four and twenty-five tells us, *"Wherefore the law was our schoolmaster to bring us unto Christ, that we might be justified by faith. But after that faith is come, we are no longer under a schoolmaster."*

Faith is more than just believing that there is a God in Heaven. Faith is believing that when God speaks through His Word, that every word is true and that He will fulfill that promise no matter how the circumstances may look. When He said *"neither is there salvation in any other: for there is none other name under Heaven given among men, whereby we must be saved"* (Acts 4:12), do you believe it to be true, or do you challenge it?

Faith is believing that when God speaks through His Word, that every word is true and that He will fulfill that promise no matter how the circumstances may look.

When He said that *"except a man be born of water and of the Spirit, he cannot enter into the kingdom of God"* (John 3:5), do you think that is was only for a generation long ago? How about when He said *"if any man have not the Spirit of Christ, he is none of his"* (Romans 8:9), do you justify a different way of receiving His Spirit than recorded within the pages of the scripture? A faith like Abraham's will hear the Word of God and trust his life to God by obeying that Word. This type of faith is what Paul was speaking of when he wrote, *"That the blessing of Abraham might come on the Gentiles through Jesus Christ; that we might receive the promise of the Spirit through faith"* (Galatians 3:14).

In the beginning years of the Church, it was difficult for the Jew to accept the fact that God could save a non-Jew (a Gentile). When in Cornelius' house, Peter finally made this comment, *"Of a truth I perceive that God is no respecter of persons: But in every nation he that feareth him, and worketh righteousness, is accepted with him"* (Acts 10:34-35).

Two thousand years later, the predominately Gentile Church may say that they totally agree with Peter, yet being absolutely transparent, we still struggle with understanding whom God is willing to save. We may be actually shocked at whom God is trying to save in our communities. Some pastors may think that God can absolutely save the drunkard or the drug addict but could never change the heart of the homosexual or the prostitute. Some pastors may be fearful of having a ministry that reaches out to the gay community because they would not want a person that struggles with "those kinds of sexual desires" but then do not have a second thought about reaching out to a sexually active "straight" young adult.

We may be actually shocked at whom God is trying to save in our communities.

To understand the *"mystery of His Will"*, we must realize that God is wanting to save the broken- hearted, the outcast, the incarcerated, the sexually active, the sexually inactive, the married, the divorced, the young and the old. The mystery of His Will is God reaching into other cultures, other religions, other nationalities, and other skin colors to bring His wonderful saving grace into their lives. What would you do if God was dealing with the heart of one of the members of the Muslim Brotherhood, (or similar organization) or an area gang and would lead them to your church? How would you respond if God was dealing with the heart of a practicing warlock and they showed up in your Sunday morning service? You never know whose heart God is dealing with right now. Acts chapter nine begins with these words, *"And Saul, yet breathing out threatenings and slaughter against the disciples of the Lord"* (verse 1). Then we see that Saul is in Damascus and

God is wanting to convert him into one of the greatest soul winners for Jesus Christ. Yes, you never know whose heart God is dealing with right now! Do not let someone else's sin, past or present, stop you from sharing the gospel with them.

What would you do if God was dealing with the heart of one of the members of the Muslim Brotherhood, (or similar organization) or an area gang and would lead them to your church?

As Paul was speaking to the people in the Corinth Church, he reminds them that they were once sinners. Paul even begins to list what they were once involved in:

> *Know ye not that the unrighteous shall not inherit the kingdom of God? Be not deceived: neither fornicators, nor idolaters, nor adulterers, nor effeminate, nor abusers of themselves with mankind, Nor thieves, nor covetous, nor drunkards, nor revilers, nor extortioners, shall inherit the kingdom of God. And such were some of you: but ye are washed, but ye are sanctified, but ye are justified in the name of the Lord Jesus, and by the Spirit of our God.* (1 Corinthians 6:9-11)

Notice that Paul not only reminded them of what they used to be, but also what God has changed them into. Whose heart is God working on right now? People are not always happy in their sin and are often what God calls the "broken-hearted". The broken-hearted may put on a happy face in front of other people, but when they face themselves in the mirror at home, they know their own brokenness, and many are desiring to give up their lifestyle for something that can heal their heart. They may be the ones praying today that God sends you to tomorrow. God is no respecter of persons!

The broken-hearted may put on a happy face in front of other people, but when they face themselves in the mirror at home, they know their own brokenness, and many are desiring to give up their lifestyle for something that can heal their heart.

While Peter was hesitant to go preach to Cornelius, it was somewhat of a different story for the disciple sent to preach to Saul when he was blinded on the road to Damascus. These next verses tell us of the Lord's encounter with Ananias in Acts 9:10–18:

> *And there was a certain disciple at Damascus, named Ananias; and to him said the Lord in a vision, Ananias. And he said, Behold, I am here, Lord. And the Lord said unto him, Arise, and go into the street which is called Straight, and enquire in the house of Judas for one called Saul, of Tarsus: for, behold, he prayeth, And hath seen in a vision a man named Ananias coming in, and putting his hand on him, that he might receive his sight. Then Ananias answered, Lord, I have heard by many of this man, how much evil he hath done to thy saints at Jerusalem: And here he hath authority from the chief priests to bind all that call on thy name. But the Lord said unto him, Go thy way: for he is a chosen vessel unto me, to bear my name before the Gentiles, and kings, and the children of Israel: For I will shew him*

how great things he must suffer for my name's sake. And Ananias went his way, and entered into the house; and putting his hands on him said, Brother Saul, the Lord, even Jesus, that appeared unto thee in the way as thou camest, hath sent me, that thou mightest receive thy sight, and be filled with the Holy Ghost. And immediately there fell from his eyes as it had been scales: and he received sight forthwith, and arose, and was baptized.

Notice how the Lord had given Saul a vision of a man named Ananias coming in and laying his hands upon him for the healing of his eyes. Of course, God was also working upon Saul's heart to be converted, but all of that was happening ever before Ananias agreed to obey God and go preach to a man that had a reputation of being a terrorist to the Christian Church. Yes, there may be someone trying to get out of their misery of sin who is praying right now, and God may be trying to move on a believer's heart to speak a word of hope to that person.

There may be someone trying to get out of their misery of sin who is praying right now, and God may be trying to move on a believer's heart to speak a word of hope to that person.

As I mentioned at the beginning of this chapter, several of the "mysteries" mentioned in the New Testament come together to show that God had originally worked through the Jewish people, but His intent was always to bring the Gentile people into the promise of salvation. Here are a few of the other references to the mystery of the Gentiles becoming fellow-heirs:

For I would not, brethren, that ye should be ignorant of this mystery, lest ye should be wise in your own conceits; that blindness in part is happened to Israel, until the fulness of the Gentiles be come in. And so all Israel shall be saved: as it is written, There shall come out of Sion the Deliverer, and shall turn away ungodliness from Jacob: For this is my covenant unto them, when I shall take away their sins. (Romans 11:25-28)

Now to him that is of power to stablish you according to my gospel, and the preaching of Jesus Christ, according to the revelation of the mystery, which was kept secret since the world began, But now is made manifest, and by the scriptures of the prophets, according to the commandment of the everlasting God, made known to all nations for the obedience of faith . . . . (Romans 16:25-26)

In reference to the sixteenth chapter of Romans and the verses quoted above, Paul makes two statements that I would like to emphasize. First, he makes a reference to *"my gospel"*. Paul is not trying to indicate that his gospel is different from the Apostles' gospel. As Paul was writing to the Church at Galatia, he gives his testimony of his conversion. From Galatians 1:13 through Galatians 2:10, Paul also tells of how he went to Jerusalem and *"communicated unto them that gospel which I preach among the Gentiles"* (Galatians 2:2). The outcome of this communication is found in verse nine of chapter two:

And when James, Cephas, and John, who seemed to be pillars, perceived the grace that was given unto me, they gave to me and Barnabas the right hands of fellowship; that we should go unto the heathen, and they unto the circumcision.

In other words, Paul was given approval by the elders in the Jerusalem Church to preach unto the heathen (the Gentiles) while the other Jewish preachers tried to reach the Jewish people.

Of course, the other of Paul's statements I want to emphasize is, *"according to the revelation of the mystery, which was kept secret since the world began, But now is made manifest, and . . . made known to all nations for the obedience of faith"* (Romans 16:25-26). The mystery which was kept secret since the world began is what God revealed to Paul and now was being made known unto all the world, not just the Jewish world. Every nation will hear the gospel of Jesus Christ!

Knowing the sheer magnitude of reaching the Gentile world with the gospel, Paul made this request to the Ephesian Church:

> *Praying always with all prayer and supplication in the Spirit, and watching thereunto with all perseverance and supplication for all saints; And for me, that utterance may be given unto me, that I may open my mouth boldly, to make known the mystery of the gospel, For which I am an ambassador in bonds: that therein I may speak boldly, as I ought to speak.* (Ephesians 6:18-20)

As Paul wrote to the Church at Colossi, he again asks for prayer for his burden to reach the world:

> *Continue in prayer, and watch in the same with thanksgiving; Withal praying also for us, that God would open unto us a door of utterance, to speak the mystery of Christ, for which I am also in bonds: That I may make it manifest, as I ought to speak.* (Colossians 4:2-4)

*This mystery which was kept secret since the world began is God reaching into all cultures, all religions, and all nationalities to bring His wonderful saving grace into their lives. Regardless of a person's gender identity, sexual activity, broken relationships or moral failures, God is trying to reach those that have not given their hearts over to Jesus Christ. If you have never experienced salvation as taught by the early church and as evidenced in the book of Acts, please go to **www.Just1God.org** and click on the tab, "Church Search". There will be websites of organizations that can help you find churches in your specific area that are still being faithful in the stewardship of this powerful mystery revealed to the early church.

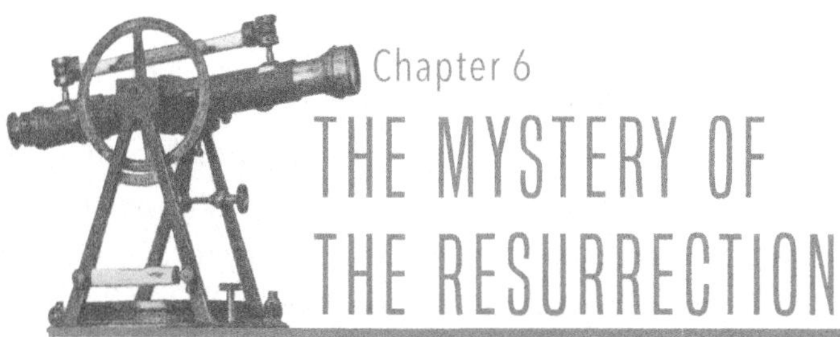

Chapter 6

THE MYSTERY OF THE RESURRECTION

"Now this I say, brethren, that flesh and blood cannot inherit the kingdom of God; neither doth corruption inherit incorruption. Behold, I shew you a mystery; We shall not all sleep, but we shall all be changed, In a moment, in the twinkling of an eye, at the last trump: for the trumpet shall sound, and the dead shall be raised incorruptible, and we shall be changed. For this corruptible must put on incorruption, and this mortal must put on immortality. So when this corruptible shall have put on incorruption, and this mortal shall have put on immortality, then shall be brought to pass the saying that is written, Death is swallowed up in victory. O death, where is thy sting? O grave, where is thy victory? -- The sting of death is sin; and the strength of sin is the law. But thanks be to God, which giveth us the victory through our Lord Jesus Christ. Therefore, my beloved brethren, be ye stedfast, unmoveable, always abounding in the work of the Lord, forasmuch as ye know that your labour is not in vain in the Lord."

1 CORINTHIANS 15:50-58

As we begin this chapter looking at the mystery of the resurrection, it is important to note that it is not uncommon for people to use words to describe particular thoughts that are not actually translated as such from the original biblical text. For example, people talk about the *Apocalypse*. What do we think of when we say the word "Apocalypse"? Maybe the end of the world? Maybe World War III and worldwide disaster?

If you do an internet search, "Where in the Bible does it talk about the Apocalypse", the typical internet search might refer you to Revelation chapter six, where it talks about the four horsemen and the great earthquake, and every mountain and island being moved out of their places. But nowhere in chapter six is the Greek word "Apocalypse". However, there are movies that Hollywood has put out about an "Apocalypse" that seem to follow this script. I ask you, have they really made movies about the "Apocalypse"? The word itself is found only one time in the book of Revelation, but where is it? It is found in Revelation chapter one, verse one: *"The Revelation of Jesus Christ, which God gave unto him, to shew unto his servants things which must shortly come to pass; and he sent and signified it by his angel unto his servant John"* (Revelation 1:1).

The word *Revelation* comes from the Greek word *apokalypsis.* We call this last book of the Bible the book of Revelation. But it could just as well be called the book of the Apocalypse. *Strong's Concordance* gives us the meaning of this Greek word as "a disclosure, a revealing, or a manifestation." To show the possible misunderstanding of this Greek word, it is used in Luke 2:32 when the child Jesus was being blessed by Simeon. He describes the child as *"A light to lighten the Gentiles, and the glory of thy people Israel." Lighten* comes from the Greek word *apokalypsis.* In other words, Jesus is a light to be disclosed or manifested unto the Gentiles.

I am only illustrating this to show that we sometimes get a thought in our minds about a certain event that may not be the intent of the writer within the pages of the Bible. Then at other times, the Bible clearly brings forth an idea that is very hard for us to comprehend because we have never seen anything like the concept happen before. This chapter is about a mystery that Paul speaks of here and in other places of the New Testament. Yet, it can be hard for some people to accept the concept only because it defies our human understanding. There are many things written within the pages of the Bible that defies our understanding. There was a metal axe head that floated in water at a prophet's command. There was a sea that parted for a nation to escape captivity. There were people raised from the dead. There were blind eyes that were opened. There were healings that took place with just a spoken word. And now, Paul is telling about something that is beyond our ability to explain how it will happen. Many people cannot scientifically explain how the light bulb comes on when we flip a light switch. They may be able to repeat explanations they learned in school, but do not truly understand it. Yet, they can turn on a light switch and expect light to come forth. Just because we cannot explain scientifically how in the twinkling of an eye our bodies will be changed from mere flesh and blood to a body like the resurrected body of Jesus Christ, does not mean that God cannot do it.

This chapter is about a mystery that Paul speaks of here and in other places of the New Testament. Yet, it can be hard for some people to accept the concept only because it defies our human understanding.

Most people refer to this event that Paul discusses as *the rapture* of the Church. Although Paul never uses the Greek word for *rapture* in any of his writings, as he teaches this subject to the Church at Thessalonica, he does refer to believers being caught up to meet Jesus in the air (1

Thessalonians 4:17). What Paul teaches is the same concept of a rapture that is being taught in churches today. In bringing forth this doctrine, it is not my intent to discuss the "timing" of a rapture of the Church; many other writers can discuss and debate that subject. However, Paul tells us that one of the mysteries that was once hidden and now made known to the Church is the fact that the dead in Christ, and those that are alive in Christ, will be "caught up" to be with Jesus. One of the most blessed hopes that the Christian holds onto is the idea that we will be changed from a corruptible body into an incorruptible body. This is the eternal experience that is spoken of in the Bible when it says *"And God shall wipe away all tears from their eyes; and there shall be no more death, neither sorrow, nor crying, neither shall there be any more pain: for the former things are passed away"* (Revelation 21:4).

Paul is revealing a mystery to the believers at Corinth about something that is promised to happen at a future date. In order to understand much of this, I will briefly review some of the Greek words that are used here to describe this mystery. In verse fifty, Paul parallels flesh and blood (our bodies) with the word *corruption*. The Greek word Paul uses for corruption is *phthora. Strong's Concordance* defines this word as "decay, or that which is subject to corruption or is perishable". We realize that our fleshly bodies are perishable. When our bodies are placed in a grave, the flesh will decay and return to the dust (Genesis 3:19).

Paul then parallels inheriting the Kingdom of God with inheriting incorruption. The Greek word used for incorruption is *aphtharsia. Strong's Concordance* defines this word as "incorruptibility, unending existence, or immortality". While our fleshly bodies have limited "shelf life" upon this earth, our resurrected bodies will have an unending existence. Our life upon this earth has been compared to a vapor that appears for a little time and then vanishes away (James 4:14), and compared also to grass that flourishes and then dies (Psalm 90:5, James 1:11). While our time on this earth is short, eternity lasts forever. The most important thing that you can do upon this earth is to make sure you are ready for the rapture of the Church.

In 1 Corinthians 15:51, Paul declares, *"Behold, I shew you a mystery; We shall not all sleep, but we shall all be changed."* Having already understood by previous chapters that a mystery is something that was once hidden but now revealed, Paul reveals to us the doctrine of the resurrection, or the changing of our bodies from something that can decay to an immortal body that will live throughout eternity. The Greek word that he uses for sleep is the word *koimao*. *Strong's Concordance* defines this word as "to put to sleep, to slumber, or to die". The word literally means to lay out prostrate; so, therefore, we can see it being used as a sleeping position, or to lay out for burial position. Fourteen out of the eighteen times the word *koimao* is used in the New Testament, it refers to death. When Paul says that we *"shall not all sleep"*, he is telling us that the change that is going to occur will happen to some people before death comes to them. We think of a resurrection as something that happens to one that is already dead. The change that Paul is instructing us in is going to happen to the *"dead in Christ"* and to those that are still living. The change will transform a human body from something that is capable of decaying to something that will never decay or die.

Paul reveals to us the doctrine of the resurrection, or the changing of our bodies from something that can decay to an immortal body that will live throughout eternity.

Paul addresses this same doctrine of the resurrection/rapture in his letter to the Church at Thessalonica. His letter lends great detail of what is to come:

> *But I would not have you to be ignorant, brethren, concerning them which are asleep, that ye sorrow not, even as others which have no hope. For if we believe that Jesus died and rose again, even so them also which sleep in Jesus will God bring with him. For this we say unto you by the word of the Lord, that we which are alive and remain unto the coming of the Lord shall not prevent them which are asleep. For the Lord himself shall descend from heaven with a shout, with the voice of the archangel, and with the trump of God: and the dead in Christ shall rise first: Then we which are alive and remain shall be caught up together with them in the clouds, to meet the Lord in the air: and so shall we ever be with the Lord. Wherefore comfort one another with these words.* (1 Thessalonians 4:13-18)

Even though most of what is spoken here is self-explanatory, there are two words I wish to clarify.

The first word is the word *prevent*. We often think of the word in the English language to mean to stop or to inhibit. The Greek word means to be beforehand, or to precede. If you think of that meaning and then look at the word *prevent* as a root word with a prefix on the front of it, it makes more sense. *Pre-* is a prefix which means "before" or "prior to" and can be understood in a word like "preschool". The word *vent* means an opening in which something can escape, such as steam, air, etc. So, Paul is telling the Church that those that are still alive at the coming of the Lord shall not be taken out of this world before the dead in Christ. As the dead are taken up, then those that are alive and remaining will be caught up to be with the Lord. Even a split second of departure beforehand would satisfy the truth of this teaching. But the dead in Christ will not be left behind.

That brings us to the second word I want to clarify. Paul uses the Greek word *harpazo*, which is translated in the KJV Bible as "caught up". *Strong's Concordance* defines this word as "to seize, to catch away or up, to pluck, to pull, or to take (by force)". Although the word *rapture* is not found in the Greek New Testament or in the King James Version of the Bible, scripture does teach that a rapture of the Church will take place. In 1 Thessalonians 4:13-18 and in 1 Corinthians 15:50-55, Paul refers to the fact that those that are dead and those that are living will experience a transformation from an earthly body to a heavenly body. The only way that a live person can be united in the clouds with Jesus is for his body to leave this earth by some supernatural means. Two other references are made in the Bible of a person that was alive and left this earth (besides Jesus being taken up in Acts 1:9). In Genesis 5:23-24, scripture tells us, *"And all the days of Enoch were three hundred sixty and five years: And Enoch walked with God: and he was not; for God took him."* The other reference is in 2 Kings 2:11. The scripture describes Elijah's departure:

> *And it came to pass, as they still went on, and talked, that, behold, there appeared a chariot of fire, and horses of fire, and parted them both asunder; and Elijah went up by a whirlwind into heaven.*

The only way that a live person can be united in the clouds with Jesus is for his body to leave this earth by some supernatural means.

These two men did not die before being taken up to be with God.

Continuing now with the supernatural event of the changing of our bodies from earthly corruptible to Heavenly immortality, we will examine 1 Corinthians 15:52. Paul tells us, *"In a moment, in the twinkling of an eye, at the last trump: for the trumpet shall sound, and the dead shall be raised incorruptible, and we shall be changed."* The Greek word that is translated into the word *moment* is *atomos. Strong's Concordance* defines this as "uncut, by implication, indivisible, or an atom of time". We get the English word *atom* from this Greek word. Paul then adds a second designation of a quickness of time by adding the phrase, *"in the twinkling of an eye". Strong's Concordance* defines *twinkling* as "a jerk of the eye". Imagine something about to hit a person in the face. The eyelid can flinch quicker than we can command it to close. Paul is telling us that this catching away will happen in the quickest time that we can imagine.

When Jesus tells of how two individuals will be working in the field and one will be taken and the other left (Matthew 24:40), realize that the coming of the Son of Man and the gathering together of His Church will be so quick that we will not have time to prepare our souls for His coming as the event happens. We must be ready every day. Matthew chapters twenty-four and twenty-five warn us of signs of the end times and how some will not be prepared for His return. Matthew chapter twenty-five tells of the ten virgins (signifying purity), but five entered in and five were not prepared by having enough oil in their lamps to make it through the night. Since oil has been used in the Bible to signify the Spirit of God, this parable indicates that they were not ready spiritually.

How many Christians are going through their daily routine without even thinking that today might be the day that our Lord returns for His Church? How many Christians today will neglect to read their Bible or neglect to even pray? Many people give the excuse that they do not have the time to do things like this, but the truth is our time is being taken up by many earthly cares. The parable of the ten virgins said that they all slumbered and slept. Those two words mean that they all were nodding and laid down to rest. Parables are used to liken something people could understand to something that they may not have understood in any other teaching. They are meant to show an earthly example to compare it to the Kingdom of God. The Church needs to wake up from their slumber and realize that we have been given the stewardship of the mysteries of God so we can reach a lost and dying world. The Church needs to realize that this mystery of a catching away (rapture) of the dead and the living still needs to be proclaimed to this lost world before the time that it actually happens. The Church needs to wake up. The Church needs to believe that Jesus is coming back for His Bride. We must make the choice every day to be ready.

The Church needs to wake up from their slumber and realize that we have been given the stewardship of the mysteries of God so we can reach a lost and dying world.

---

*With all of the signs of the end that are coming upon this world in our present age, today is not the day to be procrastinating with your salvation. If you have never experienced the powerful infilling of the Holy Ghost as mentioned in the book of Acts chapter two, evidenced by speaking in other tongues, or, if you have never been baptized in the name of Jesus Christ for the remission of your sins, please go to **www.Just1God.org** and click on the tab titled "Church Search". There will be websites of organizations that can help you find churches in your specific area that are still being faithful in the stewardship of this powerful mystery revealed to the early church.

Chapter 7

THE MYSTERY OF INIQUITY

"Now we beseech you, brethren, by the coming of our Lord Jesus Christ, and by our gathering together unto him, That ye be not soon shaken in mind, or be troubled, neither by spirit, nor by word, nor by letter as from us, as that the day of Christ is at hand. Let no man deceive you by any means: for that day shall not come, except there come a falling away first, and that man of sin be revealed, the son of perdition; Who opposeth and exalteth himself above all that is called God, or that is worshipped; so that he as God sitteth in the temple of God, shewing himself that he is God. Remember ye not, that, when I was yet with you, I told you these things? And now ye know what withholdeth that he might be revealed in his time. For the mystery of iniquity doth already work: only he who now letteth will let, until he be taken out of the way. And then shall that Wicked be revealed, whom the Lord shall consume with the spirit of his mouth, and shall destroy with the brightness of his coming: Even him, whose coming is after the working of Satan with all power and signs and lying wonders, And with all deceivableness of unrighteousness in them that perish; because they received not the love of the truth, that they might be saved. And for this cause God shall send them strong delusion, that they should believe a lie: That they all might be damned who believed not the truth, but had pleasure in unrighteousness."

2 THESSALONIANS 2:1-12

Paul's instructions to the Thessalonians were necessary because there were some men teaching that the Day of Christ was *"at hand"* (2 Thessalonians 2:1-2). Paul is reassuring the saints that certain things must happen before the day of Christ takes place. Paul reminds them that he had taught on these events when he was there with them in person. Paul says in verse five, *"Remember ye not, that, when I was yet with you, I told you these things?"* As Paul is speaking about these future events of the end times, he refers to the mystery of iniquity. As we look at this mystery, we will also look at the teaching that Paul is presenting here that explains and demystifies this thing called iniquity.

While the meanings of the words *sin* and *iniquity* are almost the same, the Greek uses different words for each. The Greek word for *sin* means to miss or wander from the path of uprightness and honor, or to violate God's law. The Greek word for *iniquity* means the condition of being without law, because of ignorance of it or because of violating it. Iniquity is more of a condition or character of lawlessness or wickedness within the heart. Sin can refer to one single violation of God's Word, but iniquity will usually point to a lawless or defiant character.

The mystery that Paul brings out here is the mystery of iniquity. Back in the Garden of Eden, Adam and Eve allowed sin into their lives, but Satan was the one that entered into the Garden with a lawless and defiant heart. Satan's whole intent in the Garden (and ever since then) was to make man distrust the truth of God. The mystery of iniquity began with Satan, but Paul is defining to the Thessalonians the mystery behind Satan from the very beginning. Books could be written on why a man or a woman who knows the love and mercy of God would be willing to trade all of the riches of Heaven for a fleeting moment of sin upon this earth. Millions of Christians have undoubtedly forsaken God and all of Heaven's glory for an affair or for "thirty pieces of silver" (the love of money). The saddest part of a trade of this caliber is that usually the relationship from the affair, and the "thirty pieces of silver", do not last long in this temporary world. Heaven's glory, though, is an eternal blessing, versus an eternity in the anguishing torment of hell. Scripture poses the question, *"For what shall it profit a man, if he shall gain the whole world, and lose his own soul? Or what shall a man give in exchange for his soul?"* (Mark 8:36-37). But Paul is not referring to the mystery of why someone would make the damning trade of their soul for something so short-lived on this earth.

There is a virus of the soul that Satan infects humans with. Paul brings out one of the main symptoms of this infected soul in verse ten: *"And with all deceivableness of unrighteousness in them that perish; <u>because they received not the love of the truth</u>, that they might be saved"* (2 Thessalonians 2:10). Sin can come into one's life when one begins doubting the Word of God, such as what happened with Adam and Eve. A lawless heart comes when one does not have a love for the truth. Truth is not decided by CNN, FOX News, or any other news agency or journalist, but truth is decided by the Word of God. Truth is not even decided by a preacher. Whether you are a preacher or not, only you can decide if you want to accept what is already written in God's Word. Even someone's denial of God's Word does not negate God's Word as truth. God's Word stands as truth whether anyone believes it or not. John 17:17 says, *"Sanctify them through thy truth: thy word is truth."* Paul said that those that do not have a love for the truth will believe a lie. Scripture explains this by stating, *"And for this cause God shall send them strong delusion, that they should believe a lie: That they all might be damned who believed not the truth, but had pleasure in unrighteousness"* (2 Thessalonians 2:11-12).

Truth is not decided by CNN, FOX News, or any other news agency or journalist, but truth is decided by the Word of God.

Jesus will reach out to the lost just as He washed Judas' feet and allowed him to partake of the last supper with Him. Jesus allowed Judas to take communion with Him. God does not want any to perish. Yet, if you do not have the love for the truth, then the infection of iniquity will set in. The Old Testament prophet Jonah spoke these words as he ran from his stewardship and eventually found himself in the belly of the great fish, *"They that observe lying vanities forsake their own mercy"* (Jonah 2:8).

Paul tells us how a human can become exposed to this deadly virus of the soul. One simply does not have a love for truth. Without a love for truth, one's heart is unprotected, and it is then possible to receive every lie that Satan brings their way. As the writer of Proverbs personifies wisdom in chapter one, it is as if God parallels this to those that turn from God's knowledge and correction:

> *Turn you at my reproof: behold, I will pour out my spirit unto you, I will make known my words unto you. Because I have called, and ye refused; I have stretched out my hand, and no man regarded; But ye have set at nought all my counsel, and would none of my reproof: I also will laugh at your calamity; I will mock when your fear cometh; When your fear cometh as desolation, and your destruction cometh as a whirlwind; when distress and anguish cometh upon you. Then shall they call upon me, but I will not answer; they shall seek me early, but they shall not find me: For that they hated knowledge,*

> *and did not choose the fear of the Lord: They would none of my counsel: they despised all my reproof. Therefore shall they eat of the fruit of their own way, and be filled with their own devices. For the turning away of the simple shall slay them, and the prosperity of fools shall destroy them. But whoso hearkeneth unto me shall dwell safely, and shall be quiet from fear of evil.* (Proverbs 1:23-33)

Returning to 2 Thessalonians, as Paul mentions the mystery of iniquity, please understand that this spirit goes much deeper than the decisions that a human being makes concerning their salvation. The spirit of iniquity has affected billions of people over the course of history. This is not something that can die with a generation, and it cannot be birthed by a movement. The mystery that Paul is speaking of has existed in Satan since his fall from God's authority. The fall of Satan, whose original Biblical name was Lucifer, can be found in Isaiah chapter fourteen. I have also heard this passage referred to as "The Five 'I Wills' of Satan":

> *How art thou fallen from heaven, O Lucifer, son of the morning! how art thou cut down to the ground, which didst weaken the nations! For thou hast said in thine heart, I will ascend into heaven, I will exalt my throne above the stars of God: I will sit also upon the mount of the congregation, in the sides of the north: I will ascend above the heights of the clouds; I will be like the most High. Yet thou shalt be brought down to hell, to the sides of the pit.* (Isaiah 14:12-15)

Because Satan wanted to be like the Most High, the mystery (the Hidden Secret) of iniquity refers to his desire to have mankind worship him instead of God. If Satan could not have mankind literally bow and worship himself, his second desire would be that mankind not worship

God either. While God's love for us keeps God reaching for lost humanity, Satan's desire stems from an intense hatred for anything that God loves. John 10:10 clarifies, *"The thief cometh not, but for to steal, and to kill, and to destroy: I am come that they might have life, and that they might have it more abundantly."* With Satan tempting mankind to be disobedient to God, man would fall out of God's mercies and favor if man sinned.

The Word of God has always been a target of Satan's attack to destroy man's relationship with God. In the Garden, the first words recorded of Satan speaking to mankind were, *"Yea, hath God said, Ye shall not eat of every tree of the garden?"* (Genesis 3:1). If we ever begin to doubt God's Word, or if we are ignorant of God's Word, then it is easy for Satan to lead us into the "sin" part of violating God's Word. Therefore, it is imperative we learn the mysteries that have been given to us as stewards. It is the Church's responsibility as stewards to reach a lost and dying world. It is the Church's responsibility to preach the TRUTH, and not preach deluded, watered down doctrines that spill over into error. We must love the truth enough to make changes in our lives so we can follow the Word and then share the Word with others. We become unprofitable servants if we bury the truth that we have been given. Proverbs 23:23 charges us to *"Buy the truth, and sell it not; also wisdom, and instruction, and understanding."*

The Word of God has always been a target of Satan's attack to destroy man's relationship with God.

By using the term "mystery of iniquity", Paul is referring to a force that has been working without the knowledge of others that is bringing about disobedience or doubt to the truth of God's Word. It began with the fall of Satan but has been active throughout the history of mankind. It is still active today, even within the Church. This lawlessness is not referring to lawlessness to man's laws, but a lawlessness to God's Word. There are churches, congregations, and individual Christians who no longer want to acknowledge truth or follow God's Word. Paul warns of this happening inside the Church in his second letter to Timothy:

> *For the time will come when they will not endure sound doctrine; but after their own lusts shall they heap to themselves teachers, having itching ears; And they shall turn away their ears from the truth, and shall be turned unto fables.* (2 Timothy 4:3-4)

For this type of spiritual virus to germinate, our world is not void of churches, but instead, it is infected with diseased churches and contaminated doctrines. We live in a day when churches are embracing a partial gospel and false doctrines, and when churches do not want to preach about sin or repentance. The churches can be small churches or mega churches. There is a prominent mega church in America that has thirty thousand in attendance on Saturday night and then again on Sunday morning with a pastor who has said that he does not want anyone to feel bad about their lifestyle. That same preacher could not say that a non-believer in Christ would go to hell. He does not want to offend Muslims, Hindus, atheists, and so forth.

For this type of spiritual virus to germinate, our world is not void of churches, but instead, it is infected with diseased churches and contaminated doctrines.

That is the kind of preaching that is infiltrating the pulpits of churches that will bring about the lawlessness to God's Word without doing away with churches. Scripture speaks of these times, saying, *"This know also, that in the last days perilous times shall come. For men shall be lovers of their own selves . . . Having a form of godliness, but denying the power thereof: from such turn away"* (2 Timothy 3:1-5).

Paul knew that false doctrines would enter the Church. Satan hates truth and he works hard to remove truth from the Church. There will not be any preachers standing up on a Sunday morning and telling his listeners that what he is about to preach is false doctrine. If a person does not love the truth, then he will believe a lie and will accept the lie as truth that he is standing on. What many people are really standing on are traditions that have been taught from years and generations past, not truth. Tradition should not be allowed to destroy the love for truth.

Paul begins 2 Thessalonians 2:1 by addressing the coming of our Lord Jesus Christ and the gathering of the Church unto Christ. This is referring to the rapture of the Church out of this world. In the first letter to the Thessalonians in chapters four and five, Paul had written no less than seventeen verses concerning the rapture. With the confusion that developed from other teachers coming after Paul, teaching that the tribulation was at hand, Paul addresses this issue again in his second letter.

The Day of Christ that is being referred to is the time when God says it is His turn to step forward and allow His full wrath to be poured out upon this earth. It is the period of time often referred to as the tribulation or Daniel's seventieth week (a period of sevens—Daniel chapter nine). According to 2 Thessalonians 2:3, the Day of Christ cannot come until two things happen. First, there is a falling away, forsaking or apostasy from truth. The "falling away" does not mean a mass exodus of Christians leaving the Church. The Greek word used for "falling away" is *apostasia. Strong's Concordance* defines this word as "defection from truth". As scriptures repeatedly point out, there will be many false teachers coming into the Church and they will be leading people into false doctrines.

The "falling away" does not mean a mass exodus of Christians leaving the Church. The Greek word used means "defection from truth".

The forsaking of the truth by the world and within the Church has already been presented here. Paul addresses this in his letter to Titus:

> *Not giving heed to Jewish fables, <u>and commandments of men, that turn from the truth</u>. Unto the pure all things are pure: but unto them that are defiled and unbelieving is nothing pure; but even their mind and conscience is defiled. They profess that they know God; but in works they deny him, being abominable, and disobedient, and unto every good work reprobate.* (Titus 1:14-16)

The second thing that must happen is a certain Person is revealed—the man of Perdition, the incarnation of evil, the Antichrist. This human being will be taken over by Satan as no individual ever was before. The Greek word used here for *revealed* is once again from a word we already studied in the last chapter of this book, but now is with a different tense. The word is *apokalyptō. Strong's Concordance* tells us that the meaning is to "lay open what has been veiled or covered up, to disclose what before was unknown". Satan, because of his desire to be like the Most High, is always trying to imitate God.

God was manifested in the flesh through the birth of Jesus Christ. Satan is now going to manifest himself through the flesh of an Antichrist. He is going to be revealed in the last days. But there has been something that has been hindering him from being revealed in his full evilness and hatred of God. In verses six and seven of 2 Thessalonians, Paul uses these phrases, *"now ye know what withholdeth that he might be revealed in his time"* and *". . . only he who now letteth will let, until he be taken out of the way."* Something is stopping or holding back this evil from being loosed into the world. And then he that is holding back Satan will be taken out of the way.

The same Greek word is used in verses six and seven and is translated as *withholdeth* and *letteth*. The Greek word is *katechō* and *Strong's Concordance* defines it as "to hold down, or to hinder the course or progress of". I do not believe a country, even the United States of America, has the power to hold back the unleashing of the Antichrist. If Paul was referring to the Church (the truth believing, spirit-filled Church, not the people falling away) as that which holds back the evil of the Antichrist, the feminine pronoun of "she" would have been used for the "Bride of Christ" instead of "he". The only other thing that has the power to hold back evil like this is the Spirit of God. A masculine pronoun would be used in reference to the Spirit as it is used here. God could remove His redeeming spirit from the earth as the times of the Gentiles are fulfilled (Luke 21:24) and grace comes to a close. Daniel's seventieth week indicates a covenant being established with Israel, not from the Messiah, but from the one that came and destroyed the city in the sixty-ninth week and cut off the Messiah. According to Revelation, the covenant will be broken after three and a half years. Since the Messiah is not a covenant breaker, the covenant of Daniel's seventieth week will be with the revealed Antichrist. Once again, because of Satan's desire to be like the Most High, he is always trying to imitate God. This time, Satan (the Antichrist) wants to enter into a covenant like God has with Israel. Then, according to Daniel, in the midst of the seven years, he shall cause the sacrifice and the oblation to cease.

The Church established by grace is wedged in between the sixty-ninth and the seventieth week of Daniel, from the time the Messiah was cut off to when the covenant is confirmed. IF Paul is telling us that it is God's Spirit that is holding back the revealing of the antichrist, and His Spirit is to be removed from the earth, then what happens to the true Spirit-filled Church? Will the Spirit-filled people of God be left here on this earth without the Spirit of God? Paul addresses this in Romans 8:11: *"But if the Spirit of him that raised up Jesus from the dead dwell in you, he that raised up Christ from the dead shall also quicken your mortal bodies by his Spirit that dwelleth in you."* To show the usage of the word translated as *quicken* in other places in the Bible, Jesus said, *"For as the Father raiseth up the dead, and quickeneth them; even so the Son quickeneth whom he will"* (John 5:21). At some point in this seven year period God will rapture the Church and only those filled with His Spirit will be a part of it.

The Church established by grace is wedged in between the sixty-ninth and the seventieth week of Daniel, from the time the Messiah was cut off to when the covenant is confirmed.

Do you love the TRUTH of God's Word enough to seek it out for your life and then obey it? Your answer to that question will determine whether you will be saved or not. Your answer to that question will determine where you spend eternity!

*As we see hatred building up against the preaching of truth . . . As we see our cities being set on fire and looted . . . As we see churches being shut down, labeled as being non-essential while abortion clinics remain open, labeled as being essential . . . As we see Christians not coming back to worship services as church doors open . . . Let us understand that we are living in rapidly changing times that are becoming more turbulent every day. If you have been having a hard time living for God when things were easy to live for Him, what will happen to your commitment now? The prophet Jeremiah penned the following words that parallel our day:

If thou hast run with the footmen, and they have wearied thee, then how canst thou contend with horses? and if in the land of peace, wherein thou trustedst, they wearied thee, then how wilt thou do in the swelling of Jordan? (Jeremiah 12:5)

If you have left the Church in the past and have not rejoined one . . . or if you are a member of a church that does not preach the gospel of repentance, complete water baptism in the name of Jesus Christ for the remission of your sins, receiving the Holy Ghost evidenced by speaking in other tongues, and living a Christian life of separation from sin, please go to **www.Just1God.org** and click on the tab, "Church Search". There will be websites of organizations that can help you find churches in your specific area that are still being faithful in the stewardship of these powerful TRUTHS revealed to the early church.

Chapter 8

THE MYSTERY OF THE GREAT WHORE

"And there came one of the seven angels which had the seven vials, and talked with me, saying unto me, Come hither; I will shew unto thee the judgment of the great whore that sitteth upon many waters: With whom the kings of the earth have committed fornication, and the inhabitants of the earth have been made drunk with the wine of her fornication. So he carried me away in the spirit into the wilderness: and I saw a woman sit upon a scarlet coloured beast, full of names of blasphemy, having seven heads and ten horns. And the woman was arrayed in purple and scarlet colour, and decked with gold and precious stones and pearls, having a golden cup in her hand full of abominations and filthiness of her fornication: And upon her forehead was a name written, Mystery, Babylon the Great, the Mother of harlots and abominations of the earth. And I saw the woman drunken with the blood of the saints, and with the blood of the martyrs of Jesus: and when I saw her, I wondered with great admiration. And the angel said unto me, Wherefore didst thou marvel? I will tell thee the mystery of the woman, and of the beast that carrieth her, which hath the seven heads and ten horns. The beast that thou sawest was, and is not; and shall ascend out of the bottomless pit, and go into perdition: and they that dwell on the earth shall wonder, whose names were not written in the book of life from the foundation of the world, when they behold the beast that was, and is not, and yet is. And here is the mind which hath wisdom. The seven heads are seven mountains, on which the woman sitteth. And there are seven kings: five are fallen, and one is, and the other is not yet come; and when he cometh, he must continue a short space. And the beast that was, and is not, even he is the eighth, and is of the seven, and goeth into perdition. And the ten horns which thou sawest are ten kings, which have received no kingdom as yet; but receive power as kings one hour with the beast. These have one mind, and shall give their power and strength unto the beast. These shall make war with the Lamb, and the Lamb shall overcome them: for he is Lord of lords, and King of kings: and they that are with him are called, and chosen, and faithful."

Revelation 17:1-14

God wants the Church to understand the end times and the book of Revelation, but "End Time Prophecy" is not the purpose of this book. The purpose of this book is to show the Church what we are responsible for in our stewardship when it comes to the mysteries of God. However, you would be amazed at all of the signs that are being fulfilled in our generation today - the earthquakes, the wars and rumors of war, nation against nation and kingdom against kingdom, the famines and pestilences, droughts, floods, sin abounding, the love of many waxing cold, etc. As you read this chapter, understand that this chapter is not intended to be a lesson about the end times, but about a mystery that God saw fit to put into the book of Revelation. Once again, the Bible gives the Church enough clues to understand what is being talked about while giving the unbeliever enough vagueness to keep them in the dark. The unbelievers just see symbolism they cannot understand. This particular mystery is different from the other mysteries of the Bible. All of the other mysteries were things that had been "kept secret since the world began" and then revealed to the Church. This mystery would be something that would happen at some point in time after the beginning of the Church age, although it does have roots from a previous period in time.

This mystery would be something that would happen at some point in time after the beginning of the Church age.

John the Revelator leaves us clues, or prophetic signs, that will identify for us this Mystery Harlot of Revelation chapter seventeen. As we begin to look at the prophetic signs and evidences, let me say that I believe that they all point to the Roman Catholic Church. But in defense of people who are Catholic, I would also like to say that I believe that Roman Catholics make the best converts into the truth of the Bible because of how devoted they are to what they believe. I would also like to say that as we look at the signs that John leaves to us, it is important to realize that the book of Revelation was written before the "Catholic" Church was ever established in Rome. God has a way of knowing things that will happen even before they happen.

The first clue to the identification of Mystery Babylon is the label that God puts on her. God allows John to label her as "The Great Whore" (Revelation 17:1). I think this is of great importance that God puts this particular label upon her. After all, what is the basic definition and understanding of a whore? *Merriam-Webster Dictionary* defines a whore as "a person who engages in sexual intercourse for pay". In addition to this understanding, a whore never enters into a permanent commitment to the man in marriage, nor ever takes on the name of the man. It was the Roman Catholic Church in the Council of Constantinople and the Council of Nicea that gelled together a doctrine of a Trinitarian God that the Roman Catholic Church follows today. It was also the Catholic Church that stopped following the apostles' teaching of water baptism by complete immersion and from using the name of Jesus in baptism by substituting the titles of Father, Son, and Holy Ghost. Remember that God is the one that calls the mystery Babylon a Great Whore. A whore is one that never takes on the name of the man or submits to him. The whore is only interested in a relationship with the man for some type of profit but will never submit to his commandments. For example, Acts 10:48

says, *"And he commanded them to be baptized in the name of the Lord . . . ."* Biblical water baptism involves both the complete submersion into water and taking on the name of Jesus – the only *"name under Heaven given among men whereby we must be saved"* (Acts 4:12). The Catholic Church does neither.

A whore is one that never takes on the name of the man or submits to him.

The next prophetic sign given to us to identify Mystery Babylon is that she sits upon many waters (also found in verse one of Revelation chapter seventeen). When the angel tells John of the mystery of the woman, the angel says in verse fifteen, *"And he saith unto me, The waters which thou sawest, where the whore sitteth, are peoples, and multitudes, and nations, and tongues."* God is letting us know the definition of the "many waters". The woman is not limited to one region of the world, but easily crosses borders and boundaries. When you look at the Catholic Church, you can easily see that this description fits her. If this was the only sign that fit her, I would easily discard it since you could say the same thing about Christianity in general, or even major international companies like Coca-Cola, Amazon, Apple, etc. But when all of the signs seem to point to the same entity, then we better try to understand who it is and what the signs literally mean.

The next prophetic sign is from verse two of Revelation chapter seventeen, and it allows us to see that the kings of the earth have committed fornication (spiritual idolatry) with her. Throughout history, there are accounts of kings that have had to get the blessing of the Pope in order to reign, to marry, or even to go to war. Once again, it points to the Roman Catholic Church.

Also, in Revelation 17:2, the scripture identifies her by the fact that *"the inhabitants of the earth have been made drunk with the wine of her fornication." Strong's Concordance* says that this can mean metaphorically "one who has shed blood profusely". Although that may not seem to make sense at this point in her description, I am going to keep that idea out there for you to think about and I will get back to it. However, just thinking about the ordinary sense of the phrase, most would understand it as when a person becomes intoxicated, they will lose their senses in making good decisions. Scripturally speaking, a person can become so indoctrinated (intoxicated) that even when shown what the Bible actually says, they will refuse truth because of what they have been taught all of their lives. I will return to the metaphorical possibility from *Strong's Concordance* when we see the signs mentioned in verse six of Revelation chapter seventeen.

Scripturally speaking, a person can become so indoctrinated (intoxicated) that even when shown what the Bible actually says, they will refuse truth because of what they have been taught all of their lives.

Three prophetic signs are issued in Revelation 17:4, the first of which is *"the woman was arrayed in purple and scarlet colour . . . ." The Catholic Encyclopedia* tells us that bishops wear purple garments and cardinals wear red garments in official gatherings. Of course, the primary color of the priest and Pope is white, but the Bible is giving us clues to guide us to the right interpretation of this mystery woman. If you would do a search on the internet for pictures of gatherings of bishops and cardinals at a Roman Catholic official assembly, you would see the brilliant colors of purple and scarlet. Again, any one of these signs taken by themselves would not be of very much significance, but when you see that these signs were written long before the start of the Roman Catholic Church, then it really stands out as a warning.

The second prophetic sign issued in Revelation 17:4 is that the woman is *"decked with gold and precious stones and pearls . . . ."* Newscasters repeatedly report that the embellished clothing worn by the Pope on special occasions is richer in gold and jewelry than any worldly crown. Also, the Pope's crown on display in the Vatican Museum is beyond ability to put a price on. Where else in our world can we see these signs such as the colors and riches like those mentioned in this chapter of the book of Revelation? If all of the archdioceses of the world were to be pooled together in wealth, it would definitely be worth more than any other multinational business.

The third prophetic sign given in Revelation 17:4 is that the woman has *"a golden cup in her hand full of abominations and filthiness of her fornication . . . ."* Up until modern times, the chalice used in communion (cup of the mass) was required to be gold plated inside if it was not made entirely of gold. The Catholic Church suggests that Catholics take communion every time they go to Mass, which is held every week. If the sign of the golden cup is in reference to the cup of communion used by the Roman Catholic Church, then the prophetic sign of verse four is saying that the Great Whore's golden cup of communion is full of abominations and filthiness of her fornication.

The terms *"abominations"* and *"fornication"* can refer both to detestable sexual acts and to the worship of idols. Communion is a very solemn act of examining oneself as one remembers the reason for the Lord's death. The first book of Corinthians describes the damnation incurred when one does not cleanse oneself before communion:

Wherefore whosoever shall eat this bread, and drink this cup of the Lord, unworthily, shall be guilty of the body and blood of the Lord. But let a man examine himself, and so let him eat of that bread, and drink of that cup. For he that eateth and drinketh unworthily, eateth and drinketh damnation to himself, not discerning the Lord's body. (1 Corinthians 11:27-29)

Communion is a very solemn act of examining oneself as one remembers the reason for the Lord's death.

This prophetic sign is not suggesting that communion is wrong, but that the Great Whore is performing communion without cleansing itself of abomination.

Another prophetic sign given to us so we can determine the identity of the Great Whore is in Revelation 17:5. It reads, *"And upon her forehead was a name written, MYSTERY, BABYLON THE GREAT, THE MOTHER OF HARLOTS AND ABOMINATIONS OF THE EARTH."* The actual mystery that is being revealed here to the saints of the New Testament Church is the fact that this coming organized spiritual movement labeled as the Great Whore actually began with the religious worship that started in Babylon. I ran across the following quote many years ago while I was reading the footnotes in *Dake's Bible*. Finnis Jennings Dake wrote a commentary on the entire Bible. This is found in his Large Note Edition, copyrighted July 1981, New Testament "Notes on Revelation Continued", page 309, column 1:

According to Hislop's 'The Two Babylons', which quotes 260 sources, the ancient Babylonian cult, started by Nimrod and

> his queen, Semiramis, spread among all nations. The objects of worship were the Supreme Father, the Incarnate Female, or the Queen of Heaven, and her Son. The cult claimed the highest wisdom and the most divine secrets. Besides confession to priests, there were many mysterious rites. Julius Caesar became the head of the Roman branch of the Babylonian Cult in 63 B.C. Other emperors held the office until 376 A.D. when the emperor Gratian, for Christian reasons refused it because he saw that Babylonianism was idolatrous. Demasus, the bishop of the Christian Church at Rome was elected to the headship in 378 A.D. and from here on, Babylonianism and organized Christianity became one. The rites of Babylon were soon introduced into the Christian Church. Heathen temples were restored, beautified and their rituals encouraged. Worship and veneration of images, saints, relics, private confession, penances, scourgings, pilgrimages, sign of the cross, Christmas, Lady Day, Easter, Lent, and other pagan rites and festivals, little by little, became a part of Christian worship.

While I am not trying to prove or support Dake's theology or Hislop's book, the quote may point out history that shows why the Church in Rome was led to clear departures from the Word of God. If the spirit of Babylon from the Old Testament was accepted into the Church at Rome, then all references to the abominations and fornications are definitely exposing spiritual idolatry.

But also notice that Revelation 17:5 says that the mystery harlot is referred to as the "Mother of Harlots". This is referring to all of the offspring churches that follow the same type of doctrinal error that denies the name of Jesus in the work of salvation that takes place in water baptism. Even some writers within the Roman Catholic

Church have throughout history urged Protestants to return to the "Mother Church". Most Protestant churches similarly deny submission to the command to be baptized by complete submersion and applying the name of Jesus in baptism (not taking on the name of the man who they are in relationship with). I do not mean to be harsh to the Catholic or to the Protestant believers, but to be a steward of the mysteries of God, we must stand for the truth revealed to the early church and recorded in the Word of God. It is not time to "Come back to Mother", but time to come back to the truth of the Word of God.

"Mother of Harlots" is referring to all of the offspring churches that follow the same type of doctrinal error that denies the name of Jesus in the work of salvation that takes place in water baptism.

Another prophetic sign given to identify the Great Whore is found in Revelation 17:6. John tells us that he saw "the woman drunken with the blood of the saints, and with the blood of the martyrs of Jesus". I had mentioned earlier that *Strong's Concordance* says that the phrase "the inhabitants of the earth have been made drunk by the wine of her fornication" (Revelation 17:2), can mean metaphorically "one who has shed blood profusely". Now we see a sign of being "*drunken with the blood of the saints*" (Revelation 17:6). Both the Roman Catholic and certain of the Protestant denominations have been guilty of persecuting Christians that turn from the indoctrination of their particular beliefs. The Roman Catholic Church has killed millions who have tried to follow the teachings of the Bible, labeling them as heretics.

No one could ever be able to count the total number of Christians slaughtered throughout the centuries.

William Tyndale was strangled and burnt for translating the Bible into English and printing it. This was his only crime that brought the death penalty. John Bunyan, who wrote *Pilgrim's Progress*, wrote it during his twelve years in prison. His crime was that he refused to get a license from the state Church to preach the gospel. Followers of the system of the Great Whore had become so indoctrinated that they believed they were doing God a great service by killing the "heretics" (those that did not believe or follow the errors of the Mother of Harlots).

Followers of the system of the Great Whore had become so indoctrinated that they believed they were doing God a great service by killing the "heretics" (those that did not believe or follow the errors of the Mother of Harlots).

The last prophetic sign which I want to explicate is found in Revelation chapter seventeen verses nine and eighteen. John tells us in verse nine that *"The seven heads are seven mountains, on which the woman sitteth."* Then in verse eighteen, John lets us know that *"the woman which thou sawest is that great city, which reigneth over the kings of the earth."* A city that sits on seven mountains. The Greek word for *mountain* is also translated twenty-one times in the New Testament as the word *hill.* Rome is called "the city on seven hills". Google the phrase and you will see Rome. And during the time of John's writing, Rome reigned over many of the kings of the earth. Later, so did the Roman Catholic Church. Coincidence or not, God prophesied these signs of the Great Whore ever before the Roman Church headquartered itself in Rome.

*This chapter is not intended to slam Catholics or Protestants. But God wanted this mystery to be revealed to followers who desire to be true to God. As mentioned, I have seen Catholics make the best converts because they understand the concept of devotion. But the Catholic indoctrination is damning, as it leads a believer into the traditions of men and not of God. My prayers are truly in earnest that Catholics and Protestants alike can be led to read the Bible with an open heart. Please go to **www.Just1God.org** and click on the tab, "Church Search". There will be websites of organizations that can help you find churches in your specific area that are still being faithful in the stewardship of this powerful mystery revealed to the early church. I further trust that these churches listed will have some type of Bible Study available to teach to you privately as you take your journey to freedom and salvation. Paul made a statement about Israel in Romans 10:2 that I believe can also be said about Catholics: *"For I bear them record that they have a zeal of God, but not according to knowledge."*

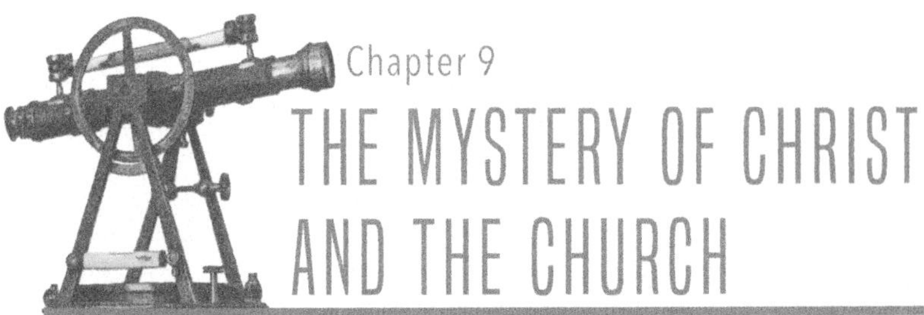

Chapter 9

THE MYSTERY OF CHRIST AND THE CHURCH

"Wives, submit yourselves unto your own husbands, as unto the Lord. For the husband is the head of the wife, even as Christ is the head of the church: and he is the saviour of the body. Therefore as the church is subject unto Christ, so let the wives be to their own husbands in every thing. Husbands, love your wives, even as Christ also loved the church, and gave himself for it; That he might sanctify and cleanse it with the washing of water by the word, That he might present it to himself a glorious church, not having spot, or wrinkle, or any such thing; but that it should be holy and without blemish. So ought men to love their wives as their own bodies. He that loveth his wife loveth himself. For no man ever yet hated his own flesh; but nourisheth and cherisheth it, even as the Lord the church: For we are members of his body, of his flesh, and of his bones. For this cause shall a man leave his father and mother, and shall be joined unto his wife, and they two shall be one flesh. This is a great mystery: but I speak concerning Christ and the church. Nevertheless let every one of you in particular so love his wife even as himself; and the wife see that she reverence her husband."

EPHESIANS 5:22-33

Paul speaks in several places in his epistles about marriage, the abstaining from marriage or the authority of the unbetrothed girl before marriage. However, this is the first time that Paul compares the union between a man and a woman with the union that exists between Christ and the Church, and then calls it a mystery. In Ephesians 5:31, Paul makes the statement about the man leaving his father and his mother and being joined with his wife and the two becoming one. It is upon the conclusion of this statement that Paul makes the comment that *"This is a great mystery"* (verse 32). Incidentally, Paul uses the Greek word *mega* again concerning this mystery (see chapter four of this book). However, notice that Paul then directs the reader to the understanding that this *mega mystery* is not really about the union of the man and the woman, but about Christ and the Church. Paul explains, "*This is a great mystery: but I speak concerning Christ and the church*" (verse 32). The true mystery is the fact that Jesus Christ has joined Himself with the Church and the two have become one.

Paul directs the reader to the understanding that this* mega mystery *is not really about the union of the man and the woman, but about Christ and the Church.

In the last century, there has been a great movement to prove that women are just as smart and competent as men, but, in all reality, the intelligence battle is not what Paul is trying to establish in this writing. In the verse right before this passage about comparing marriage to Christ and the Church, Paul makes a statement in Ephesians 5:21 that should explain more about his focus: *"<u>Submitting yourselves one to another</u> in the fear of God."* In *Strong's Concordance*, the definition of the Greek word *hypotasso*, being translated into the KJV word *submitting* that is used here and in verses twenty-two and twenty-four as *submit* and *subject, Strong's Concordance* tells us, "In non-military use, it was a voluntary attitude of giving in, cooperating, assuming responsibility, and carrying a burden." It really has nothing to do with who is the brightest or most capable. It has to do with the placement of a certain order or responsibility.

Whether the husband "rules the roost" or the wife "rules the roost", understand that God will hold the husband responsible according to what Paul is saying. Even if a mutual agreement has been made within a household for the woman to make final decisions, the order arranged by God places the accountability upon the husband. Think of a CEO allowing his or her directors, who may even be smarter in their areas of expertise, to make all of the decisions in a corporation. However, the ultimate accountability comes back on the CEO if something fails. Furthermore, if the man is not following Christ spiritually, and, therefore, not the spiritual leader of the home, God will still hold him accountable, even though he is AWOL from his spiritual duties. In this case, the woman is making the spiritual decisions in her life by still serving God, while the husband is in dereliction of his duties.

An interesting observation about the twelve verses that reveal this mystery to the Church is that there are only three brief references to the wife's role in the marriage. The references in chapter five of Ephesians are found in the following verses: v.22 submit (remember the definition in *Strong's Concordance* – a voluntary attitude of giving in, cooperating, assuming responsibility, and carrying a burden), v.24 liken yourself to the Bride of Christ, and v.33 to reverence (or respect) your husband. That is it. Everything else in the twelve verses concerning this mega mystery is about the responsibilities of the man as Paul observes the love that Jesus Christ had for the Church and commands the husband to have that type of love toward his wife.

God is setting order and responsibility in the family just like He set order in the Church. In the Church, Jesus Christ is the head, or the one that makes the final decision. Paul is clear that this is not a master / slave arrangement in the Church, nor is it in the home. In a master / slave arrangement, love does not have to exist at all. But Paul reasons that love radiated from Jesus Christ to the Church, and this same type of love must proceed from the husband to the wife for the marriage to be truly blessed.

Paul reasons that love radiated from Jesus Christ to the Church, and this same type of love must proceed from the husband to the wife for the marriage to be truly blessed.

In Ephesians 5:25, Paul writes, *"Husbands, love your wives, even as Christ also loved the church, and gave himself for it . . . ."* The Greek word for *love* that is used here is *agape*. The Greek language has given us several words that have been used throughout history that have been translated as love. Some of them are *agape*, *phileo*, *thelo*, *storge*, and *eros*. Some of these words, such as *eros*, in which we get the English word "erotic" from, were not used in the New Testament but were available for use during the time of the New Testament writings. When Paul gave the commandment to the husband to love his wife, he does not use the Greek word *eros* to indicate lustful desires, nor did he use the Greek words *phileo* or *storge* to imply a love of a family. Instead, Paul uses the Greek word *agape* for the type of love a husband is to bestow upon his wife.

Preachers have often said that *agape* love is the strongest type of love that exists. Yet, the love for family (*phileo* or *storge*) has caused fathers and mothers to run into burning buildings to try to save a child that is trapped inside, often perishing in the attempt. Fathers and mothers have often given their lives in the possible exchange to spare their child. For most fathers and mothers, they would not have to give a second thought about giving their life for a child. Before the New Testament, *agape* love would not have been considered a powerful type of love. *Agape* is a chosen love to commit to a person, not because they are family (*phileo*) and not because they are beautifully attractive (*eros*), but a choice made in someone's life to love another. With *agape*, love is not required or even expected. Not many people would give their life for a total stranger. So, what is it that makes the *agape* love so powerful? It is the teachings of the New Testament that made this *agape* love the most powerful type of love. As Jesus was teaching His disciples in John 15:13, He said, *"Greater love hath no man than this, that a man lay down his life for his friends."*

This is what makes John 3:16 so powerful. It says, *"For God so loved the world, that he gave his only begotten Son, that whosoever believeth in him should not perish, but have everlasting life."* God did not have to love the world. He could have dispensed punishment and judgment, which would have been fair since the wages of sin is death (Romans 6:23).

Again, this *agape* love only becomes such a strong love because it is a chosen love that commits to a person, not because they are family and not because they are beautiful, but a choice to love and to sacrifice. We need to realize something else about this powerful type of love that Jesus Christ was willing to give for His Bride. It was given before any love was being given in return. For example, Romans 5:6-8 lets us know this about His love:

> *For when we were yet without strength, in due time Christ died for the ungodly. For scarcely for a righteous man will one die: yet peradventure for a good man some would even dare to die. But*

God commendeth his love toward us, in that, while we were yet sinners, Christ died for us.

Understand it this way, before we loved Him, He loved us. So, this is Paul's commandment to the husband of the home—Love your wife even if you do not feel respect from your wife. Then Paul compares the *agape* love the husband should have for the wife to the love that Christ has for the Church. This is the most important part of this passage. Husbands can sometimes get obsessed on the "wives . . . submit" part. But Jesus gets obsessed on what *agape* love does in a relationship. This is expressed in the following four verses:

Husbands, love your wives, even as Christ also loved the church, and gave himself for it; That he might sanctify and cleanse it with the washing of water by the word, That he might present it to himself a glorious church, not having spot, or wrinkle, or any such thing; but that it should be holy and without blemish. So ought men to love their wives as their own bodies. He that loveth his wife loveth himself. (Ephesians 5:25-28)

Husbands can sometimes get obsessed on the "wives . . . submit" part. But Jesus gets obsessed on what **agape** ***love does in a relationship.***

Christ wanted a Church that was without spot, without wrinkle, without blemish and living a holy life. How many of you could do that without Jesus Christ in your heart? How many of you could do it without the Holy Ghost? Anybody??? The law was our schoolmaster. It came to teach us. It was a lot of words and commandments. But could anybody ever live holy and follow every commandment in the Old Testament? The same thing could be said as we enter into the New Testament. Could the Church ever love Christ the way that God wants us to without receiving His Spirit within our hearts? It took Jesus Christ dying for us and then infilling us with His Spirit before we could ever get close to the mark of holy living. His love for us and Him giving himself for us was so He could sanctify and cleanse the Church with the washing of water by the Word.

Paul is comparing that kind of love with what the man should have for his wife. How does that look in actual living? First, I will tell you what it does not look like. It does not look like the man sitting around and saying, "Woman, get me some coffee. Woman, make me some grub. Woman, why ain't my clothes washed yet?" The marriage is not intended to be a master / slave arrangement.

So, what does it look like? It looks like the *agape* love that Jesus Christ gave for His Bride. For the man to see and feel the respect and obedience in the home, he must become the spiritual defender of the home. He is going to have to die out to the carnal side of his life. He is going to have to be the spiritual leader in prayer, Bible reading, worship, and in demonstration of a godly attitude in all things. If the husband does not die to the carnal side of his life, but instead opens a door of sinfulness, and opens a door for immoral spirits to come into the home, it will demolish the spirit of submission from the wife and wreak havoc on his marriage.

There is one book that I recommend on this topic of Ephesians chapter five. The title is *Love and Respect* by Emerson Eggerich. Some may find it to be a very hard read because of the length and content, but Eggerich's teaching on the husband loving the wife and the wife respecting the husband is great. Men, create within your home the very thing that Christ desires within His Church. And it starts with your holiness . . . your consecration . . . your lifestyle of purity . . . your power in the Spirit.

But understand that if you miss the Christ / Church parallel in this passage, you will miss everything about the great mystery that Paul is bringing forth. He tells us, *"This is a great mystery: but I speak concerning Christ and the church"* (Ephesians 5:32). When we look at the marriages that end in divorce or even the marriages that are dysfunctional and are only remaining because of convenience, we could ask the question of how similar this is to the Bride of Christ not having "a voluntary attitude of giving in, cooperating, assuming responsibility, and carrying a burden" to Christ.

With this being one of the last chapters of this book, has there been mysteries presented that you are not willing to follow? Jesus, the head of the Church, said, *"And why call ye me, Lord, Lord, and do not the things which I say?"* (Luke 6:46). When we read through Ephesians chapter five, realizing that the mystery is really concerning Christ and the Church, there are two observations to be made. First, in looking at what Jesus Christ has done for His Bride, we realize just how AMAZING Christ's love is for us! But the second observation is that the Bride's obedience and submission to Christ is often very dismal.

*What about you? Have you submitted to the desires of our Lord Jesus Christ? Have you repented of any immoral thoughts or lifestyles that you may have allowed to be harbored within your life? Have you been baptized in the name of Jesus Christ for the remission (or removal) of your sins? Have you received the infilling of His Holy Spirit, evidenced like in the book of Acts, speaking in other tongues? Have you shut the door to sinfulness and immoral spirits in your heart? Have you made a commitment to prayer, Bible reading, worship, and developing a godly attitude? If you are ready to make a life-changing commitment to God and are not currently attending a church that believes and teaches the truths that have been presented in this book, please go to **www.Just1God.org** and click on the tab, "Church Search". There will be websites of organizations that can help you find churches in your specific area that are still being faithful in the stewardship of all these powerful mysteries revealed to the early church. May God bless you as you make your journey on the road of righteousness.

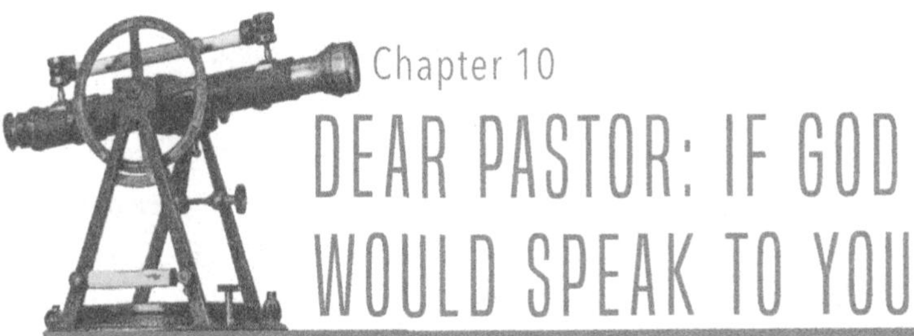

Chapter 10

DEAR PASTOR: IF GOD WOULD SPEAK TO YOU

"The mystery of the seven stars which thou sawest in my right hand, and the seven golden candlesticks. The seven stars are the angels of the seven churches: and the seven candlesticks which thou sawest are the seven churches."
REVELATION 1:20

While the earlier mysteries that have been discussed in this book have dealt with either previously hidden knowledge of God given to the church so they could reach a lost world or a revelation of a future religious system (now revealed), this mystery involves God sending messages to individual churches. While many pastors pray that God would speak to them, few would ever pray for a rebuke from God when He speaks. Yet, if a rebuke would help save your soul or those under your care, would you readily accept the message? The mystery revealed here is the understanding that God sends angels to seven of the churches of Asia Minor to deliver such a message.

The seven stars are said to be the seven angels (or messengers) to the seven churches of Asia Minor listed in the book of Revelation. These angels are not delivering seven different gospels to the seven churches, but are messengers sent to deliver a message from Jesus. The churches listed in the book of Revelation could refer to seven periods of church history, or to seven types of assemblies which could be found in the last days before Jesus returns. Since the writer is not clarifying this, it is not my intention to speculate his meaning. The writer's intention may have been to address the issues of seven churches that were existing in his present day. It is clear, though, that the angels are the messengers to a particular church. These angels were to present the errors and/or accolades of a particular church. One church, Ephesus, had a problem with departing from their first love. (Revelation 2:1-6) We can only speculate what this first love may have been. It could be they departed from loving the truth of God's Word. It could be that they departed from the worship of God Himself. Or maybe, they have departed from the love of evangelizing a lost and dying world. Whatever this love may have been, unless they repented, Jesus was ready to remove their candlestick out of its place. This is a reference that they would no longer be considered a saved church before the eyes of Jesus.

While it is reassuring to know that God has sent an angel to help a church in doctrinal issues, it is sad to know that some churches will resist to the point of having their candlestick removed from God's presence.

Two other churches, Pergamos and Thyatira, had doctrinal errors which allowed sin into their belief system. (Revelation 2:12-29) While it is reassuring to know that God has sent an angel to help a church in doctrinal issues, it is sad to know that some churches will resist to the point of having their candlestick removed from God's presence. To Pergamos, Jesus even said, *"Repent; or else I will come unto thee quickly, and will fight against them with the sword of my mouth."*

(Revelation 2:16) Ephesians 6:17 allows us to know that the sword of the Spirit is the word of God. How strange it sounds to hear Jesus telling a church that He will fight them with the word of God.

Another one of the churches mentioned, Sardis, thought they were alive, but Jesus said they were a dead church (Revelation 3:1) *Strong's Concordance* tells us that the Greek word that is used for dead means, *"one that has breathed his last, lifeless"*. This may suggest to us that this church was only going through the motions of having church, showing up because of tradition, but was spiritually dead.

Another church, Laodicea, was lukewarm and thought that they did not need anything. (Revelation3:14-20) Jesus described His reaction to this church as wanting to vomit them out. They thought they were rich, but Jesus said they were poor and wretched. They were proud of their elegant dress, but Jesus said they were naked and shameful before Him. Jesus described Himself being on the outside of this church and knocking, wanting in. This church did not even know they were operating without Jesus.

Only two of the seven churches seem to have no fault mentioned—the church at Smyrna (Revelation 2:8-10) and the church at Philadelphia (Revelation 3:7-12). Notice the words that Jesus praises Philadelphia with when He says, *"thou hast kept my word, and hast not denied my name"* (Revelation 3:8). That should be the desire of every church and of every believer.

Since each of these messages are to churches, God is first and foremost addressing the leadership of these churches. The pastor of a church is the most influential person a church has to help turn the direction of a church around if they are in doctrinal error. So pastor, do you still have your first love? Do you have a love for the truth of God? Are you able to lead your congregation in establishing their love for God's truth? Are you willing to lead them in all truth? Have you allowed doctrinal errors from tradition into your assembly that are causing them to commit spiritual adultery? Do you judge your success by the number of followers you have or the size of your buildings? Have you denied the name of Jesus in water baptism? Use the litmus test of the seven angels of Revelation and their messages to determine where you are with the truths founds in the word of God while you still can.

The pastor of a church is the most influential person a church has to help turn the direction of a church around if they are in doctrinal error.

---

*While the Bible implies that angels cannot preach the message of salvation to mankind, God desires for other human beings to testify the truths found in the Bible (Acts 10:1-6). God is trying to reach into every church congregation to direct them into truth. If you are a pastor or spiritual leader within a church assembly and you have seen the truths of this book for the first time, there are preachers ready to baptize you in the name of Jesus Christ, and then you can baptize your assembly. Please go to **www.Just1God.org** and click on the tab, "Church Search". There will be websites of organizations that can help you find preachers in your specific area that can discuss leading your entire congregation into these truths.

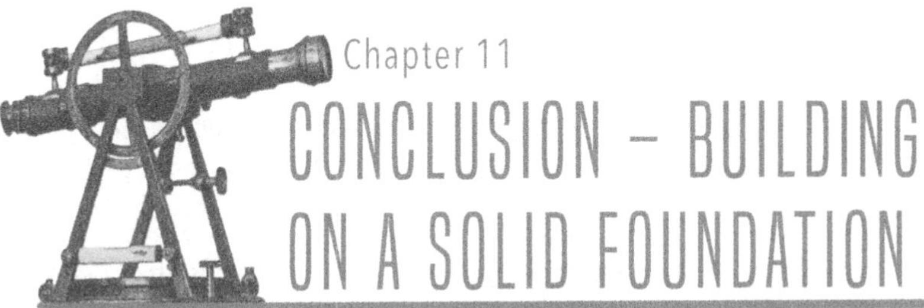

Chapter 11

CONCLUSION – BUILDING ON A SOLID FOUNDATION

"Not every one that saith unto me, Lord, Lord, shall enter into the kingdom of heaven; but he that doeth the will of my Father which is in heaven. Many will say to me in that day, Lord, Lord, have we not prophesied in thy name? and in thy name have cast out devils? and in thy name done many wonderful works? And then will I profess unto them, I never knew you: depart from me, ye that work iniquity."

MATTHEW 7:21-23

There are many churches that teach for a person to be saved, all they need to do is believe in Jesus, confess they are a sinner, accept Jesus as their personal Lord and Savior, and they are saved. Then the preacher shakes their hand as he receives them into the fellowship of other "believers". But Jesus said that *many* people will come to Him on the day of judgment thinking that they are saved, only to find themselves facing eternal damnation! Jesus informs us that there will be many people who were so assured that they were saved that they were willing to question Jesus' divine judgment. They truly believed that they were going to make it into Heaven, having faith in what they had been taught in a "Christian" church.

The word that is translated as *many* in verse twenty-two is the same Greek word used in verse thirteen of Matthew chapter seven:

> *Enter ye in at the strait gate: for wide is the gate, and broad is the way, that leadeth to destruction, and many there be which go in thereat: Because strait is the gate, and narrow is the way, which leadeth unto life, and few there be that find it.* (Matthew 7:13-14)

The warning of verses thirteen and fourteen shows that many people are walking down the wrong path of a partial Gospel that will lead to destruction. Jesus tells us that there is a path that leads to life, but only a few will find it.

The number of saved "Christians" will be small in comparison to the number of lost "Christians". How could this be possible? The very next warning Jesus gives is about false prophets appearing in sheep's clothing (Matthew 7:15-20). There will be false teachings that fail to bring people into the full knowledge of salvation. This is why there will be people who call Jesus their Lord who are not allowed into Heaven.

An argument may be made that these *many* people in Matthew 7:22 are not really Christians at all but are hypocrites and pretenders. But notice that these people obviously did not think that they were hypocrites, or else they would not have questioned Jesus in His judgment. They evidently believed that they should have made it into Heaven.

Furthermore, they were even able to bring forth an impressive list of spiritual accomplishments that they did for the Kingdom of God. These accomplishments are outlined in detail in the scriptures: *"Many will say to me in that day, Lord, Lord, have we not prophesied in thy name? and in thy name have cast out devils? and in thy name done many wonderful works?"* (Matthew 7:22). Notice that these works were all done in His name, referring to that powerful name of Jesus. They had prophesied in His name. They had cast out devils in His name. They had done many wonderful works in His name.

Interestingly enough, the Greek word translated as *"wonderful works"* in Matthew 7:22 is *dynamis* and is the same Greek word used in Acts 1:8 referring to the (dynamite) power received with the infilling of the Holy Ghost. The book of Acts says, *"But ye shall receive power, after that the Holy Ghost is come upon you: and ye shall be witnesses unto me both in Jerusalem, and in all Judaea, and in Samaria, and unto the uttermost part of the earth."* Despite the spiritual power which these people saw in their lives, Jesus still said, *"Depart from me, ye that work iniquity"* (Matthew 7:23). These sincere people were dumbfounded at the verdict given by Jesus, but nothing they could say or do could change that proclamation once their eternity had begun.

These sincere people were dumbfounded at the verdict given by Jesus, but nothing they could say or do could change that proclamation once their eternity had begun.

Regardless of the accomplishments done in the name of Jesus, there is noticeably one major statement concerning salvation that is absent from their testimony. They did not say that they were water baptized in the name of Jesus. Is water baptism in the name of Jesus really that important? Peter stood up on the Day of Pentecost in Acts chapter two and said, *". . . Repent, and be baptized every one of you in the name of Jesus Christ for the remission of sins . . ."* (Acts 2:38). It is our faith in obeying this commandment in the Word of God that brings about the removal of our sins.

Without baptism in the name of Jesus, Jesus proclaimed that they still had sin in their lives. The blood of Jesus had not covered their iniquity. They had come so far in their belief and walk in the Kingdom of God, but evidently had no knowledge of how sins are removed through baptism in the name of Jesus, or possibly, they had refused to accept it. There have been many people that have accepted Jesus as their Savior and have said the "Sinner's Prayer". Many of these people have been taught that water baptism is not important, or have been only sprinkled with water, which is not a biblical baptism.

It is important to remember that baptism means *to immerse*. Many more have been immersed in water as an act of baptism but have been baptized in the titles of the Father, Son, and Holy Ghost. Father, Son, and Holy Ghost are titles only and not the name of Jesus. According to Acts 4:12, there is only one name to be used for salvation: *"Neither is there salvation in any other: for there is none other name under heaven given among men, whereby we must be saved"* (Acts 4:12). Jesus cast out many people that called Him Lord because they never had their sins removed from their lives by water baptism in His Name.

Jesus cast out many people that called Him Lord because they never had their sins removed from their lives by water baptism in His Name.

This demonstrates two key lessons we need to learn from this dreadful scenario on the day Jesus judges mankind. First, a lack of knowledge of what is necessary to get to Heaven cannot be used as an excuse to circumvent obedience. In Hosea 4:6, God warns, "*My people are destroyed for lack of knowledge: because thou hast rejected knowledge, I will also reject thee . . . .*" Not knowing what the Bible declares does not exempt you from damnation. The second lesson is that having faith that you are saved does not make you saved. People can be absolutely convinced in their mind that they are saved but believing that you are saved does not save you.

Jesus continues to teach these very important lessons in Matthew chapter seven regarding those thinking that they were saved but were not. He proceeds to give a parable about two men that built houses:

> *Therefore whosoever heareth these sayings of mine, and doeth them, I will liken him unto a wise man, which built his house upon a rock: And the rain descended, and the floods came, and the winds blew, and beat upon that house; and it fell not: for it was founded upon a rock. And every one that heareth these sayings of mine, and doeth them not, shall be likened unto a foolish man, which built his house upon the sand: And the rain descended, and the floods came, and the winds blew, and beat upon that house; and it fell: and great was the fall of it.* (Matthew 7:24-27)

Notice that Jesus labels one man as wise and the other as foolish. The difference between the two men was whether they obeyed the Word of God or not after they heard it. The parable used in teaching this Kingdom concept is the idea of building a house. People understand that there is a lot of effort, time, and money that goes into the building of a house. Remember this as Jesus parallels the earthly building of a house with the building of our spiritual life.

The difference between the two men was whether they obeyed the Word of God or not after they heard it.

In the parable, both men built a house. But there is no indication that one man did not take as much care in the building of his house as the other. There is no indication that one man used inferior lumber to build his house. There is no indication that the two houses looked any different.

Both men had a storm hit their house. There is no indication that the storms were of different intensities. There is no indication that the men were in different parts of the country. The only difference that Jesus tells us of is the foundations that they built upon, one foundation being ROCK and the other foundation being SAND.

What is the difference between rock and sand? The Greek words that are used here do not give us much to go on. The Greek word for *rock* is *petra. Strong's Concordance* tells us that this word simply means "a (mass of) rock". The Greek word used for *sand* is *ammos. Strong's Concordance* defines this word simply as "sand (as heaped on the beach)". While the Greek does not shine much light on the difference, the fundamental usage of the two substances shows the meaning that Jesus was trying to teach. Rock is in a solid form while sand is in a granular form. Rock and sand can also come from the same basic elements. Therefore, while rock is a solid substance, sand is only grains or pieces of a substance.

Jesus used this parable with the difference between rock and sand to show why *many* people (Matthew 7:21-23) were lost. The Word of God is the Rock. Hearing the Word of God and doing the Word places everything that you build in your spiritual life upon the rock. The people that thought they were saved in verse twenty-two heard enough of the Word to call Him Lord. They heard enough of the Word to prophesy and cast out devils. They heard enough of the Word to do many wonderful works. But they had obeyed only pieces of the Word concerning their salvation. The parable shows the sad outcome of people that have spent years of their life serving in a church and building a spiritual house, only to come to Jesus in judgment and be turned away into eternal damnation. It is not what they did in their life, it is what they did not do in their life. They may have heard the Word and read the Word a hundred times in their life, but for some reason, they failed to obey the Word. Nothing they could say or do could change their judgment once their eternity had begun.

As this book comes to a close, you are on one of two foundations. If you have already heard and obeyed the Word by having faith in Jesus in His atoning work, repented of your sins, been baptized in the name of Jesus Christ for the remission of your sins, received the Holy Ghost evidenced by speaking in other tongues, and living a holy life for Him, then you are on the Rock. Now become a steward of what you have learned by bringing others to Christ with this wonderful knowledge until He comes back for His Church. You will receive a *"Well done, thou good and faithful servant . . . enter thou into the joy of thy Lord"* (Matthew 25:21).

But if you have never heard of the salvation truths brought forth in this book, or if you have not obeyed because your church teaches differently, then there is still time for you to change your foundation before you stand before Jesus in judgment. You are currently on a foundation of sand. Your spiritual house will crumble and the fall of it will be great. But you have a choice while you are still living. You could be an eleventh-hour worker before Jesus comes back (Matthew 20:1-16). Your choices today are *"Well done"*, or *"Depart from me"* (Matthew 25:21-23, 7:23). Do not find yourself dumbfounded facing eternity.

*Go today to **www.Just1God.org**. Click on the tab, "Church Search". There will be websites of organizations that can help you find churches in your specific area that are still being faithful in the stewardship of God's Truth. I further trust that a church located close to you will have some type of Bible Study available to teach to you privately as you take your journey to salvation. Our lives are like *"a vapour, that appeareth for a little time, and then vanisheth away"* (James 4:14). Do not chance an eternity in hell because of procrastination. Do it today!

AFTERWORD

Although I am a licensed, ordained minister with the United Pentecostal Church International, I have included other church organizations that preach the truths presented in this book. If for any reason, you cannot find a church near you through www.upci.org or another website listed, please email me through my website at **www.Just1God.org**. I will try to respond as quickly as I can. Your eternal salvation is very important to me and to the Kingdom of God. The Bible says we must be ". . . *warning every man, and teaching every man in all wisdom; that we may present every man perfect in Christ Jesus*" (Colossians 1:28).

God Bless,
Eric D. Smith

Made in the USA
Columbia, SC
19 February 2021

33131963R00065